Scotland Vol II

Edited by Heather Killingray

Young Writers

First published in Great Britain in 2006 by:
Young Writers
Remus House
Coltsfoot Drive
Peterborough
PE2 9JX
Telephone: 01733 890066
Website: www.youngwriters.co.uk

SB ISBN 1 84602 430 7

Foreword

Young Writers was established in 1991 and has been passionately devoted to the promotion of reading and writing in children and young adults ever since. The quest continues today. Young Writers remains as committed to the nurturing of poetic and literary talent as ever.

This year's Young Writers competition has proven as vibrant and dynamic as ever and we are delighted to present a showcase of the best poetry from across the UK and in some cases overseas. Each poem has been selected from a wealth of *A Pocketful Of Rhyme* entries before ultimately being published in this, our fourteenth primary school poetry series.

Once again, we have been supremely impressed by the overall quality of the entries we have received. The imagination, energy and creativity which has gone into each young writer's entry made choosing the poems a challenging and often difficult but ultimately hugely rewarding task - the general high standard of the work submitted ensured this opportunity to bring their poetry to a larger appreciative audience.

We sincerely hope you are pleased with this final collection and that you will enjoy *A Pocketful Of Rhyme Scotland Vol II* for many years to come.

Contents

The Poems

My Bedroom

My bedroom is a clean place
My bedroom is a neat place
My bedroom is a short place
My bedroom is a long place.

My bedroom is a posh room
My bedroom is a quiet room
My bedroom is a tidy room
My bedroom is the shiniest room.

My bedroom is the warmest room
My bedroom is the cosiest room
My bedroom is the nicest room
My bedroom is the cutest room.

My bedroom is a tower top
My bedroom is a cherry pie
My bedroom is an ice cream delight
My bedroom is a daisy petal.

My bedroom is a gold medal runner
My bedroom is a super star
My bedroom is a disco ball
My bedroom is *magnificent!*

My bedroom is *not* the neatest
But my bedroom is definitely *me!*

Demi McSporran (10)
Crookston Castle Primary School, Glasgow

Quickly

Quickly the rocket shoots up in the sky,
Quickly the bullet hit someone in the eye,
Quickly the hailstones hit the ground,
Quickly the greyhounds are running around.

Quickly the vulture swept down on its prey,
Quickly the boy fell asleep in the hay!

Lauren Thomson (10)
Crookston Castle Primary School, Glasgow

Anger

My anger comes through my skin from my heart
My blood raging . . . so grumpy.
My bad temper is so bad that . . .
No one really likes me
My blood is coming out of me so fast.

My anger is so bad
That no one stands a chance.
My blood goes faster
Than cars on the motorway.

James Campbell (9)
Crookston Castle Primary School, Glasgow

Anger

My anger is like tomato ketchup
Exploding out of the bottle.
My anger is like blood
Gushing out of my veins.
My anger is like a man
Just been denied a job.
My anger is like a boy
Just been told he cannot play the game.
But my anger is not that bad . . .
Especially *not* today!

Brandon Thomson (11)
Crookston Castle Primary School, Glasgow

Fear

My fear is like a fly in a spider's trap
My fear is like the fish in the sea
My fear is like a little insect getting lost
My fear is like a bug being washed away.

Chelsea Skilling (10)
Crookston Castle Primary School, Glasgow

My Bedroom

My bedroom is a nice place
My bedroom is a mean place
My bedroom is a messy place
My bedroom is a pretty place.

My bedroom is a perfect place
My bedroom is a tidy place
My bedroom is a Bratz place
My bedroom is a pink place.

My bedroom is a clean place
My bedroom is a garbage place
My bedroom is a gorgeous place
My bedroom is a cold place.

My bedroom is like a palace
My bedroom is like *Hell*
My bedroom is like *Heaven*
My bedroom is like a paradise.

My bedroom is a medical room
My bedroom is a gold runner room
My bedroom is a dancing room
My bedroom is a learning room.

My bedroom is a place to practise
All the things that make me *me!*

Laura McGregor (10)
Crookston Castle Primary School, Glasgow

My Bedroom

My bedroom is very untidy
It looks like a bomb has hit it.
See the pizza box melting with sog?
You taste the yuckiest pizza *ever!*
You smell the rot of the pizza too.
I can hear people shouting in the cupboard to help.
You can see the place is a real mess.

Christina Angus (10)
Crookston Castle Primary School, Glasgow

Red

Red is my blood coursing through my veins.
Red are cherries that are as sweet as can be.
Red are roses that show true love.
Red are peppers that make your mouth burn with fire.

Red is my heart that beats all day long.
Red is the pillar box that shines in the sun.
Red is a pencil that we use to colour in.
Red is a school jumper that we wear to school.

Jennifer Devoy (10)
Crookston Castle Primary School, Glasgow

Anger

My anger is like a volcano
Just about to erupt.
My anger is like a tsunami
Capsizing a large boat.
My anger is like a gigantic monster
Stomping on lots of cars.
My anger is like an insane bull
Charging at a red cape.

Steven Hannah (10)
Crookston Castle Primary School, Glasgow

Anger

My anger is a bull
Charging at a red cape.
My anger is a witch
With big rotting warts.
My anger is a speeding bullet
Just shot from a gun.
My anger is a red dragon
Breathing smoke and fire.

Ryan Skinner (10)
Crookston Castle Primary School, Glasgow

My Bedroom

My bedroom is like a rubbish bin
My bedroom is like an endless rubbish bin
My bedroom has so many . . .
Toys, clothes, it's so unreal.

My bedroom is so dirty
My mum doesn't care anymore.
My bedroom is the dirtiest
Room in the world.
My bedroom is the dirtiest
In the universe!

Luke McPhee (10)
Crookston Castle Primary School, Glasgow

Anger

My anger is like a book being slammed shut
And it feels like a hammer hitting an ant.
My anger tastes like a rotten chip
And smells like lots of dead people in a closed room.
My anger is like thunder and lightning
Rumbling high in the sky.

My anger is like a shark eating a little fish
And it feels like a dog chasing a cat.
My anger is like lots of people
Shouting at a football match!

Scott MacMaster (10)
Crookston Castle Primary School, Glasgow

Colours

Yellow is the colour of the sun in the morning
Yellow is the colour of a bun I like to eat at teatime
Yellow is the colour of Tweetie Pie who hides from Sylvester
Yellow is the colour of apple pie which I like to eat.

Chavonne Pollock (11)
Crookston Castle Primary School, Glasgow

My Bedroom

My bedroom is a tip with socks all over the place
My bedroom is not a tidy place
My bedroom cannot stay tidy
My bedroom is a tip I always say to my friends.

My bedroom is a tip with socks and clothes all over the room
My bedroom is not very tidy
My bedroom is a messssssssssss!

My bedroom is still a very good room
My bedroom is a *very big* mess
My bedroom is a *very big* tip
My bedroom is a pit of garbage
My bedroom is a bottomless pit of socks
Socks, socks and more socks!

Jade Hughes (10)
Crookston Castle Primary School, Glasgow

Colours

Blue is the sky high above my head
Blue is the colour I support the best
Blue is the colour of the deep blue sea
Blue is the colour I like the best.

Blue is the colour of a boy called Lee
Blue is the colour the dark, dark sky
Blue is the colour of the icing on my cake
Blue is the colour of my kitchen plates.

Red is the colour of a red, red rose
Red is the colour of our new school sweatshirt too!

Colours for me
And colours for you!

Jamielee Angus (11)
Crookston Castle Primary School, Glasgow

Yellow

Yellow is the colour of baby chicks born in the spring
Yellow is the colour of the sun
Yellow is the bright colour of daffodils
Yellow is the colour of cheese that I have on my toast.

Yellow are bananas which I love to eat
Yellow is the lemon which is so, so sweet
Yellow is a pineapple, juice I refuse to drink
Yellow is butter that I spread on my toast.

Jocelyn Boyce (10)
Crookston Castle Primary School, Glasgow

My Dog

My dog
Is cool, he can fetch sticks.
He can run as fast as a Ferrari
When it's trying to win.

He pretends he's dead
Fetches the paper, catches the ball.
Barks when he's hungry
Dreaming of a bone.

Wags when he's happy
Growls when he's angry
Likes when you feed him
And scratch his back.

My dog
His name is Arran
He chases dangers away
I like my dog
He's
Cool!

Mathew Howie (9)
Crosshill Primary School, Maybole

The Chiger

It's as fast as lightning
And as ferocious as a shark!
If it gets you, it will tear you
From limb to limb!

Its head is orange with black stripes
Its body is yellow with black spots
It will eat anything that moves
And can catch anything that runs!

It is the new king of the jungle
It will take down a lion with one snap of the jaw
It could even take down a buffalo
In ten seconds . . . *flat!*

It has eyes as sharp as a hawk
and if it sees you, you'll be first on the menu
For
Its
Tea!

Thomas Johnston (11)
Crosshill Primary School, Maybole

My Baby Sister

My baby sister
Crawling on the floor
You should hear her roar
Have to feed her every day
She loves to roll about and play
Cleaning bins in every way
Take her for walks in sunny May
I've to pick up everything she drops
Even though she cries a lot
I still love her
My baby sister.

Adele Templeton (10)
Crosshill Primary School, Maybole

The Haunted Bathtub

My bathtub is very spooky
I think it's alive!
I don't like my bathtub
Don't know if I'll survive.
I think it ate a sub
And now the sub is up above!

My bathtub is very creepy
And sometimes very sleepy
When you touch
You must beware
He could give you an awful scare.

My bathtub is very scary
Sometimes it is also hairy
Something else about my bathtub
It says, 'Glug!' when I pull the plug.

Christopher Rowney (9)
Crosshill Primary School, Maybole

The Monster

This monster sleeps under beds
And eats children's heads
He comes out at nights
To give children frights
If I were you
I wouldn't
Turn out
The
Lights!
He's big, fat and hairy
His teeth are real scary
His eyes are red horns on
His head
This the monster
That lives under your bed!

David Harkness (11)
Crosshill Primary School, Maybole

The Weird And Wonderful Creatures

The man who went to the jungle
Got an awful rumble.
One great big punch from the kangaroo
And splat face first into elephant poo.

The elegant model who went to the zoo
Tripped over a rock and cried, 'Boo hoo,'
She shouted, 'I've broken a beautiful nail.'
The parrot cried, 'Ow, you slimy snail!'

The scientist who went scuba-diving
Went into the water in the dark.
Before he knew his son was skiving,
He was eaten by a shark.

The family who went on a boat,
They always boast, shout and gloat.
There was a leak, they shouted, 'Bail!'
Then they were eaten by a whale.

These huge great animals
Are beautiful creatures,
But have their own
Extraterrestrial features.

Adam Copeland (10)
Crosshill Primary School, Maybole

My Dog

My dog is so cute
She plays with Dad's boot
She even likes to read my book

We like to take her for a walk
In the woods
I put up my hood and then I shout, *'Boo!'*

When I go to my bed
There's a lump that's not Ted
But it's my dog Meg.

Emma Lawrie (9)
Crosshill Primary School, Maybole

My Bed

Relaxing and warm
I lounge in my bed
I feel like I'm floating
On clouds

Comfy and cosy
Is my bed
Lovely covers
I lie under

Cuddling into my teddies
Snuggling in my bed
Gently drifting away

Snuggling warm is my cosy bed
Lovely covers all comfy and warm.
Slowly . . .
Drifting . . .
Away.

Jodie Wallace (10)
Crosshill Primary School, Maybole

Strange

Catfish are fish with heads of pussycats,
Jump out of bowls, curl up on mats.

Bullfrogs have horns and rings in their nose,
Green lanky legs, green hooves, not toes.

Horseflies are huge they *neigh and buzz*,
Bristly legs, manes, tails and fuzz.

Tiger sharks are stripy, eat fish and deer,
Run if you think they are anywhere near.

Sheep dogs are black, they *baa* and *woof,*
As soon as they're born, their wool will go poof!

Turtledoves have shells, they have wings too,
Sometimes they are silent, other times they doo.

Mairi Archbold (10)
Crosshill Primary School, Maybole

The Monster In The Cupboard

There's a monster in the cupboard, he's out to get *you!*
There's a monster in the cupboard, he's out to get *me!*
He's hairy, he's scary and he's always going, *'Boo!'*
We've locked him in the cupboard so he'll never get *free!*

He came here in ninety-seven
His egg came crashing down from Heaven.
An eye-catching bird fell in the mud
From his own planet he had been driven!

He'll shred you,
Behead you
Make a meal out of you!
He's got you in sight
Ready to bite
But I'm not concerned
It's the middle of the night!

Euan Andrew (9)
Crosshill Primary School, Maybole

Big Brother

I have a big brother I love him so
But how annoying he can be
He takes me out to fun places in his car
How funny he can be.
I call him names but he doesn't mind, sometimes.

My big brother he is a bit silly
He forgets his car keys and his mobile phone
When he leaves the house I'm glad he's gone, sometimes
But when he leaves I always miss him
And I'm very glad I have a big brother.

Helanna Cooper (10)
Crosshill Primary School, Maybole

Tigers

Tigers, tigers, they're afraid of fires
They have black stripes
Shaped like pipes
They would scare a bat
Like a bird with a cat
They have long sharp claws
Sticking out from their paws
They have long teeth
In their mouth beneath
They can certainly jump
And land with a thump
They are quick and fast
If in a race not last
You'd think they're cute
But hunters will shoot
They are very vicious
And to them you're delicious
They are orange or white
Both colours are light
They have a habitat
Just like the other cats.
You should not shun it!
It's an animal
You'll love it!

Lewis Paterson (10)
Crosshill Primary School, Maybole

Fairy

Beautiful, small
Flying, twinkling, fluttering
Magic me to fairyland please
Fairy.

Louise Thomason (6)
Cullivoe Primary School, Shetland

The Animals From Koo

Once upon a time,
In the land of Koo
Lived a rabbit, a hamster
And a kangaroo.

The rabbit hops
The hamster climbs
The kangaroo bounces
And plays the chimes.

Now this one strange day
Something weird appeared
The animals were out playing
And the hamster disappeared.

The kangaroo and the rabbit
Both shocked to their bones
Ran as fast as they could
To their telephones.

They called PC Plod
Who came as fast as he could
And hit himself on the head
With a big piece of wood.

For up in the air
Were UFOs
How they got there
No one knows.

They sent down an animal
All covered in yuck
But instead of a hamster
They sent down a duck.

And off he waddled down the lane
Never to be seen again.

Claire Morris (11)
Cullivoe Primary School, Shetland

Think

If pigs are pink
It makes you think
Are beetles black and blue?

If chocolate's brown
And wears a crown
Would you eat it with your stew?

If you can wink
It makes you think
Are monkeys intelligent too?

If sprouts are green
And really mean
Would you eat them on the loo?

If you enjoyed this rhyme
I think it's time
For you to go out and . . .
Think.

Ann-Marie Kennerley (11)
Cullivoe Primary School, Shetland

Jungle

Monkeys swinging in the trees
Parrots flying in the breeze
Giraffes with tall necks
A woodpecker that pecks
Cheetahs that run fast
Big trees that are vast
A snake that is long
And some things that pong
Elephants that are grey
And mice who like to play
The jungle is really hot
And I go there quite a lot.

Jamie Kennerley (10)
Cullivoe Primary School, Shetland

Celtic Rules

C eltic is the best team
E ver
L ucky they are because
T hey have a four-leaf clover
I think they are the best team in the world
C eltic rules!

Kristopher Jamieson (12)
Cullivoe Primary School, Shetland

The Day Has Dawned

D ragon comes to Cullivoe
R oaring with fireballs
A ngry, fearsome monster
G oing to call all
O r if we get him first we can save the land
N ever give up, be brave and take command.

Logan Spence (9)
Cullivoe Primary School, Shetland

Unicorn

Sparkly unicorn
Galloping
Running
Flying
Zooming me to the stars
Unicorn.

Ellen Severn (7)
Cullivoe Primary School, Shetland

Butterfly

Pretty wings
Flying, fluttering, twirling
Gliding beautifully through the sky
Butterfly.

Sophie Kennerley (7)
Cullivoe Primary School, Shetland

Elephants

E lephants
L ove
E ating
P rivet
H edges
A nd
N ot
T inned
S ausages.

John McLean (11)
Dalintober Primary School, Campbeltown

Love

Love is red like a big, bright rose
It feels like a pair of silky pyjamas
It tastes like a nice juicy strawberry
It smells like an enormous pear
It looks like a massive love heart
It sounds like a giant roaring
It reminds me of a big love heart.

Tamara Lafferty (9)
Dalintober Primary School, Campbeltown

Love

Love is red like a sweet-smelling rose.
It reminds me of soft, silky flower petals
And butterflies fluttering in the sun.
Love tastes like a big, slobbery cherry-flavoured kiss.
Love sounds like birds softly singing and tweeting
And a lake gently rushing by.
Love looks like a lovely boy or girl
With hearts all around.
Love feels like a velvet sheet of lavender
Or a juicy, fruity strawberry.

Chantelle Cameron (9)
Dalintober Primary School, Campbeltown

Laughter

Laughter is yellow like a beaming sun
It tastes like a very bitter lemon
It looks like a funny, super, brilliant day at a fair
It sounds like someone who's happy and full of delighted cheers
It reminds me of a remarkably entertaining party
It smells like an exceedingly nice smell of deodorant
It feels like a big heap of happiness.

Lee Allen (9)
Dalintober Primary School, Campbeltown

Fear

Fear is dark purple like a yucky monster in the closet
It tastes like rotten fish
It feels like a horrible slimy slug
It looks like an evil soul
It smells like an egg that is out of date
It reminds me of getting screamed at by ugly, mean people
It sounds like opera singers getting louder and louder.

Zoe Clayton (9)
Dalintober Primary School, Campbeltown

Darkness

Darkness is black like a big black hole
It reminds me of something evil like a hurricane
or a giant deep volcano
It sounds like a cold, high-pitched screaming going on forever
It smells like a damp dark cellar or a sewer
It tastes like cold porridge or rotten fish
It feels like wet grass or rough rocks
It looks like the gloomy dead of night closing in on me.

Philippa Fraser
Dalintober Primary School, Campbeltown

Happiness

Happiness is green like the soft sweet grass
It reminds me of a cool funfair in a sunny city
It sounds like a sweet skylark singing softly in the sky
It feels like a soft blue pillow
It tastes like the loveliest chocolate in the world
It smells like the greatest perfume in the world.

Christina Robertson (9)
Dalintober Primary School, Campbeltown

Love

Love is yellow like the bright and glittery sun
It sounds like a lovely, shining, sunny day
It reminds me of a day of running like the wind round the giant park
It feels like the most juiciest, runniest cakes
It tastes like a soft pineapple
It looks like a biscuit with a buttery, cheesy taste
It smells like mince and mashed potatoes.

Aidan McLean (9)
Dalintober Primary School, Campbeltown

A Baby Boy

He screams
He wails
He gets everything he wants
A bath
A bottle
A dummy
Though each day he'll fill your life with joy . . .
And a dirty, stinky nappy!

Lauren Wilson (10)
Dalintober Primary School, Campbeltown

Housework

We always get told to do the *dirty* dishes
We always get told to *clean* our rooms
We always get told to *clear* the table
We always get to mow the *grass*
We are never allowed to play *outside*
Housework is rubbish!

Caroline Logan (10)
Dalintober Primary School, Campbeltown

Anger

Anger is red like a dark red card
It smells like a dead rat
It sounds like a dark, evil voice
It feels like a rough, sore surface
It reminds me of a dark red planet
It tastes like a disgusting grey table
It looks like a scary devil face.

Gavin Russell (9)
Dalintober Primary School, Campbeltown

Saturday Night

S unday
A rrives
T omorrow
U ntil then I have to wait
R ain has been tipping down all
D ay
A nd
Y outh club is just starting

N oise heard for miles
I nside
G irls chasing boys
H ere is all the mischief
T earing down the walls.

Adam Kenny (10)
Dalintober Primary School, Campbeltown

The Summer Holidays

Ding-dong!
The bell rings long,
Everyone cheers as they hear
It's the summer holidays!

Grabbing their bags,
Stacking their chairs,
No time to lose
Remember it's the summer holidays!

Catching their buses
Screaming and shouting
It's the summer holidays!

Packing their suitcases
To go on holiday
But . . .
Soon it will be school again,
But never mind it's for the best!

Eva Armour (9)
Dalintober Primary School, Campbeltown

Snowdrops

I eence hid a bunch of bonny snowdrops
I brocht them in tae the hoose,
I didnae realise it was bad luck
And the next day was affa
I forget to gie them a wee drink o' watter
And fan I got up they were deid!

Morgan McIntosh (8)
Dunecht School, Westhill

My Baby Brother

I hiv a baby brother
He ae wis pulls my hair
He crals alang the fleer a day
He's wanten me tae play.

Taylor McRobb (8)
Dunecht School, Westhill

My Grunny

My grunny is an affa lass,
She canna get aboot.
She tells me stories fae a lang time ago
An' makes me laff and laff!

Emma Macaulay (8)
Dunecht School, Westhill

My Wee Sister

I hiv a baby sister,
She dribbles doon her chin
An' fan I get hame fae school and smile at her,
She gies a muckle grin.

Katie Bain (7)
Dunecht School, Westhill

All Of My Pets

The first wee pet I ever hid,
Got up and flew awa'.
An' that wis an affa day.

Then I got a dug,
He wis white, black and broon,
He wis a lot of fun,
But noo he's deid!

My goat wis a scamp,
He got oot o' the park,
So we hid tae get rid o' him!

I hinna muckle luck wi pets,
But I cannie forget my guinea pig
Who is noo still alive!

Kirsteen Hendy (8)
Dunecht School, Westhill

My Cousin's Wee Cat

My cousin's wee cat,
Is as slim as a sausage
And as bright as *marmalade.*
She brings my auntie a lovely present
And guess what?
It's a deed moosie!

Harry Taylor (8)
Dunecht School, Westhill

My Friend

My friend Melissa,
She's ae wis tellin' jokes.
She makes me laugh an affa lot,
Until I nearly choke!

Zoe Strachan (8)
Dunecht School, Westhill

Guid Doggie

I've got a wee doggie,
A spaniel, black and white,
She snoops a roon the hoose a day
And when it comes to night,
She gulps her feed in fright!

Morna Holmes (7)
Dunecht School, Westhill

My Mither

My mither rins aboot the hoose,
Like a tiny wee moose.
She likes tae hoover up food,
We dropped all ore the fleer.
She micht nae gie us any mare food,
Weel just get breid and watter!

Gavin Elrick (8) & Morven Drummond (7)
Dunecht School, Westhill

My Pussy

My puss rins aroon the hoose
Hoping it micht find a juicy moose
To hive for her tea.

Andrew Cook & Katie Campbell (7)
Dunecht School, Westhill

Oor Pets

We hiv wee hamsters and pussycats too,
We hiv dugs that bide with you.
Somebody said my hamster looks like a moose,
In its wee shabby hoose.

Ellie Nuttall & Anna Mouat (8)
Dunecht School, Westhill

War Poem

War is the colour of black and grey smoke
with a mixture of orange, yellow and red, like fire.
War is deafening and explosive bursting your eardrums
when the bombs drop on you, killing you.
All you can taste is the dust and blood
from the dead bodies scattered all around.
I'd feel scared, worried, but helpless at the same time.
You'd think a bomb is going to drop any minute now.
It reminds me of fighting, planes and Adolph Hitler
the Germans, it's not a nice thought.

Cachelle Milne (11)
East End Primary School, Elgin

War

Red like danger telling me to hide and never come back,
It's like a waste ground, everything dumped anywhere it lands.
It sounds like fireworks on November the 5th
or in music class with the drums.
It's choking innocent, innocent *people!*
It feels like the world has been torn apart.
It reminds me of the earthquakes you've heard of.
It's telling you never come back!

Stephanie Russell (11)
East End Primary School, Elgin

War

Red, red like blood of an innocent soldier lying on the floor lifeless
It's like a pit of spikes and nettles jabbing at your heart
It sounds as if bombs are dropping from the sky hitting hidden mines
Smoke choking everyone it sees and comes in its path
It feels as if razors are cutting me at every corner
This reminds me of graveyards, so many headstones.

Sean McKillop (11)
East End Primary School, Elgin

War

War is like a big black lump of tar lying on the ground,
like the dead people that have been shot.
War looks like a garbage dump,
from all the broken pieces of houses scattered all over the ground.
War sounds like Bonfire Night from far away
but it isn't making pretty patterns, it is breaking down houses.
War tastes like sorrow because of all the unhappy people,
crying for help as they are in pain.
War feels like when you are in a rain storm,
you're being tossed about and getting shot.
After war is over, it reminds me of a funeral,
there are lots of dead people lying all over the ground.
In a war and at a funeral
there are lots of dead people lying under the ground.
Everyone is upset.

Joanne Rivard (11)
East End Primary School, Elgin

Feelings Of War

War is black,
War is sour,
Think of all the people dying by the hour.

War is great,
But war is bad,
Everyone losing everything, it is so sad.

War is unhappy,
War is unkind,
All the people, sure to be losing their mind.

War is dreadful,
War is hateful,
War . . . is . . . *everything!*

India Brown (11)
East End Primary School, Elgin

War

Red like danger, awaiting me everywhere I go,
hiding in the corners, creeping under beds.
It's like a waste ground; rubbish everywhere,
as if it's a monster that will eat your belongings.
The sound is deafening, like screams of pain
coming from someone being tortured, till they go crazy.
The taste of death is everywhere I go,
like a bad odour in the air, everywhere.
I feel that I'm being torn into pieces,
I can't go on any longer.
It's like being in a never-ending nightmare,
please set me free!

Nicole Wight (11)
East End Primary School, Elgin

War

War is black like darkness you can't get away from.
It looks like red, like flaming fire.
Bombs hitting the floor and then exploding are all you can hear.
It tastes like blood dripping from your mouth in desperation.
When you're at war it feels as if you've been shot in the head.
War reminds me of death.

Haydn Thomas (11)
East End Primary School, Elgin

War

It is dark like inside a cave
It is messy like a junkyard
It is like thunder crashing
It tastes gritty like sand from the beach
It feels like being trapped like a dog in a cage
It reminds me of dead bodies
Like black bags scattered across the ground.

Alex Miller (11)
East End Primary School, Elgin

War!

War is terrifying,
War is red for danger, hurting people in every possible way.
The people worrying with no escape,
All you can see is black smoke rising from houses
And choking everyone who comes near.
War sounds like fireworks blasting off in every direction
Or shooting down from planes above.
Coldness, sadness and darkness are all things
you can taste in the war.
Everlasting horror strikes, as it runs through the veins like poison.
Everyone is so far away, you can never talk to anybody.
It's as if all your feelings have been washed away,
War reminds me of my worst nightmare.
It is my worst nightmare when everybody goes to bed at night
And never to wake again.
War is terrifying.

Abigail Rollinson (11)
East End Primary School, Elgin

War!

Watch out!
The bombs are falling,
The injured are crawling,
Watch out!
Grab a weapon and use it well,
War can be a bit like Hell,
Watch out!
The screaming now reaches my ears,
Closer and closer, death nears,
Watch out!
Smell the gas that spreads,
Watch out like I said!

Shawnie Gordon (11)
East End Primary School, Elgin

War

War is black like dark smoke
It looks red and black with flames and smoke.
You hear bangs like a thunderstorm as guns shoot
You taste the gas and petrol as the Germans drop poisonous bombs
You feel nervous, scared as you fall asleep
Wondering if you'll ever wake up again.

Ryan Thomson (11)
East End Primary School, Elgin

War

War is like black smoke choking innocent people one by one.
War looks like red-hot flames burning everything in their path.
War tastes like deadly poison,
Horrible and killing everyone in a nasty way.
War feels like a lightning storm striking down on us.
War reminds me of a graveyard
Because of all the dead people that died in the war.

Matthew Dixon (11)
East End Primary School, Elgin

Feelings Poem

I am going to the country
I am leaving my mum
My dad is in the army
I am going to the country because of the war
I am feeling very sad
When will I see them?
What will happen if the train gets bombed?
I am very scared.

Kieran Robbins (8)
Edderton Primary School, Tain

Evacuation

I feel so strange
I don't want to leave my family
My mum is crying all the time
I have to go now
I say goodbye to my family
And rush to get a seat
I squeeze to the window
No one around with smiles on their faces
I look down at my suitcase and gas mask
I'm lonely I want someone to talk to
We're here now
I wonder if they'll like me?
Will they be nice to me?
What if they beat me up?
I'm so frightened
What if I don't see my mum and dad again?
What if they get killed?
What will happen to me?

Moyra Liz As-Chainey (10)
Edderton Primary School, Tain

The Frightened Child

I stand there, frightened
Cold all over
Being bombed everywhere
I get my gas mask and my suitcase
My mom is crying to see me leaving
As she stands there sobbing
Should I be treated fair there?
Should they not care a thing
Even if I die?
It's dark and I'm lonely
As I snap the tag off.
Since I'm left
And have to sleep in a shack.

Peter Kishnah (11)
Edderton Primary School, Tain

Evacuees

I'm feeling scared,
What will I do?
I'm also feeling very blue
The sky's so dark
Not one smile on a face
The train will soon be leaving this place
I'm on the train,
I'm waving goodbye
I start to weep and fret and cry.
The feelings I have they feel so bad
I feel so very, very sad.
The train sets off,
It slowly speeds up
My mother she seems to darken up.
The place I live just fades away
We're going to live so far away.

Nina Paiva Pennick (9)
Edderton Primary School, Tain

Evacuees!

I'm feeling so scared, what will I do?
I'm also depressed and sad too.
The train arrives, I say goodbye
My family and I, we start to cry.
I get on the train and find a seat
Then my family start to weep
I wave through the window, I blow a kiss
I've always wished my life would never be like this.
All the family's sobbing and crying
I feel like the world is dying, dying.
The war is dreadful I hate it so,
I wish it never happened, I love my family
I'm going away so, so, so far away
I hate the evacuation, the war as well
I hate it! I hate it!

Shannon Ivy Sutherland (11)
Edderton Primary School, Tain

Feelings Poem

I was going to leave for the country
Was upset when I had to go
To get my clothes and my helmet,
Mum saw me off
She ran up beside the train
The train went too fast.
I looked back and I saw her,
She was crying.
I felt lonely, scared and miserable.
When I got there
I was shoved into the place where I got battered.

Everyone was lonely
They were hungry and cold.
The next day we were battered again
We were feeling so sick
My sister died.
Heaps of people died
We were in a concentration camp.

Alex Wood (8)
Edderton Primary School, Tain

Feelings Poem

My mum is crying beside me
As I was packing my bag.
She said I'll go and make your sandwich.
I was waiting, feeling sad and mad.
We went to the station and I went to the train
And I said goodbye to my mother in shame.

I got to the destination that was called Bramble Hill
And I was shuffled into a hall that I did not like at all.
I was picked at and ticked and finally I was chosen
And I was taken away to a little house in a bay.

Ross Gollan (9)
Edderton Primary School, Tain

A Wee Child

Och, I am only a wee child
And I am getting evacuated
I am in despair
What do I do?
Someone please help me
I am lonely
I am sobbing
I want my family!

I want to get back at the Germans
They're evil, they're nasty
I need to get back at them
They made me leave my family
They're the ones who caused it all
Why? Why?

I've got my suitcase and my gas mask now
I am going to the countryside
I am all mixed up in my head
What do I do?
I am furious with the Germans
And I want my mum!

Emma Beesley (10)
Edderton Primary School, Tain

Christmas Witness

It was a cold winter's night
and a special baby was going to be born.
So I flew down and caught a glimpse
of a mother screaming and shivering.
The mother of the baby was Mary,
the father was Joseph.
Mary wore a single linen, cloth robe,
and I, an angel, was wearing a soft velvet robe
rimmed with shiny gems.

Nicole Cliffe (10)
Elmvale Primary School, Annan

Mary's Story

It was a cold night,
The stars were shining like the brightness of the sun,
All I could hear were footsteps from Joseph.
I was tired and I felt like falling asleep.
Suddenly, my attention was drawn
To something in the sky - a star, I think.
The shadows were amusing when I sat
Trying hard not to fall asleep,
I could see that the donkey was very tired
But we did not have any food
As we had just travelled for miles -
We had to keep going.
I had never felt like this before,
The light was rising from the top of the hill,
As I sat thinking about what would happen.

Later, I remembered it was a long time ago,
But I was happy
That what had happened was over.

Toni Bell (10)
Elmvale Primary School, Annan

Fireworks!

Be amazed as my colours shoot out!
Watch me charge up into the sky.
See me erupt in the air.
Clap and cheer as my spectacular rubies
Fire out in the sky.
See as I brighten up the dark sky
With my sparkling diamonds,
Scream as I explode in the air.
Goodbye and farewell
As my life ends with a
Bang!

Michael Chan (10)
Elmvale Primary School, Annan

The King's Story

I was studying the stars,
As they sparkled like diamonds,
When I saw an unusually bright star.
I looked it up in a book
And I told my friends
To set off on a long journey.

Through ferocious sandstorms
And scorching desert days,
Until we reached an oasis.
There was not much to drink
And the camels constantly snorted
And the servants were muttering and moaning.

But there in front of me,
Lay the town of Bethlehem.
And there shone the star
Like a crust of emeralds,
Shining on the town
With an emerald light.

And there I stood,
Gold in my hands,
Ready to give to the King.
But of course I knew,
That gold was not worthy of the treasure of Jesus
And I, King Casper, prayed for the baby king of the world.

Jonathan Byers (10)
Elmvale Primary School, Annan

Fireworks

Stand far back as my magnificent colours
Storm into the air!
Admire my sapphire rockets
As they burst in the atmosphere!
Jump and hide from my bright emerald explosions!
Gaze into the air as I amaze you!

Nicole Shannon (10)
Elmvale Primary School, Annan

Firework

Keep back,
Be dazzled by my extraordinary colours,
Set my fuse on fire to shoot me into the sky!
As I explode, watch the ruby, sapphire,
Emerald, silver and golden sparks fly round the sky!
Jump, scream and shout as an explosion is heard,
I will terrorise your pets,
Now goodbye, I'm going to die!
Boom! Boom! Bang! Bang!

Lewis Scott (10)
Elmvale Primary School, Annan

Fireworks

Transfix your eyes to my gleaming colours
Admire my beauty as I explode in crimson and jade.
Cheer and applaud while I soar into the night sky.
Jump and run as I remind you of treachery and treason
Be afraid of my powers!
Remember me as I ascend, then perish.
Farewell.

Ashley Hollis (11)
Elmvale Primary School, Annan

Fireworks

Be dazzled by my spectacular colours,
Never take your eyes off me,
Be afraid as I scare your animals,
Look out the window,
See if you can see me,
Jump as I explode!
Until next time,
Goodbye!

Ben Morton (11)
Elmvale Primary School, Annan

Christmas Witness

Just another night, guarding the sheep,
That's all my life was.
The moon was unclear, like she was hiding from the truth
And the stars shone faintly,
All except one which was sparkling like a diamond.
It motivated me to follow and I felt myself running in its direction,
I stumbled down the steep slope and gashed my hands
I cut my bare feet on the ragged rocks
And I grazed my knees on the gravel
As I crawled into Bethlehem,
But still I travelled on.
In the deep, sleep-black sky, the star still shone
Unlike its other siblings, but this time closer,
I realised the scintillating star shone above a ragged stable,
Behind a full inn.
I burst in and collapsed onto the golden heaps of hay,
Exhausted, but with just enough energy to gaze in wonder at the newborn Jesus,
I, a normal, common shepherd witnessed the birth of Christ.

Steven Kwok (11)
Elmvale Primary School, Annan

The Angel Witness

As I'm an angel,
I had told the whole village,
Mary was going to have a baby -
Not just any baby - this was going to be a special baby -
The baby who, in the future, would perform miracles.
We were so excited, everyone was excited.
That night He was born.
As I sang in mid-air,
I watched Mary and Joseph,
I sang of my love for them,
I will remember everything that happened that night.

Rebecca Lynch (11)
Elmvale Primary School, Annan

The View

The school crouched down like a cat waiting to pounce,
The gaping goalposts bawled in wait for children
Shooting their football dinners right down their throats.
The swallows swooped down, counting the ants,
Like divers jumping into a swimming pool
In search of lost watches and rings.
The houses were standing watch
With their glow-in-the-dark eyes, that lit up in the dead of night,
The trees swayed in the wind as it howled and moaned,
The grass was like a flat piece of green paper
With early snowflakes flittering and fluttering by.
The giraffes craned their necks and peered over the gates,
At the trees making pictures with the clouds.

Saskia Ashdown (10)
Elmvale Primary School, Annan

Birth Of A King

They rode on me.
Then I heard a noise -
I looked up
It was a dull night,
There were dark grey clouds everywhere
But then there was a gush of light,
The stars came out and there were lovely white clouds.
There, I had finally got to the stable.
I couldn't believe my eyes . . .
With thin black hair and wrapped in a little brown rag,
It was the baby called Jesus.
I felt somehow so brave,
But I must admit,
The stable was a bit smelly,
I will still remember that night.

Michael Wilson (11)
Elmvale Primary School, Annan

Christmas Witness

I stood in the stable watching it all.
I saw the shepherds and the kings all crowded round.
I saw the little baby Jesus lying in the crib.
I felt hungry and cold - and grumpy
At no attention being paid to me.
I decided to sit down to have a rest
After the long trek to Bethlehem.
I heard a loud knock, as a shepherd opened the door.
I ran to Mary and sat up next to her.
I looked at the dark blue sky,
I saw the white twinkling stars
And sheep standing on the hilltop.
I stood up and knew I would always remember that day.
I am the donkey that carried Mary to Bethlehem.

Lauren Hodgson (11)
Elmvale Primary School, Annan

The Angel And The Birth

I sang for Jesus in the air with Gabriel,
My new robes encrusted with precious jewels,
My pure white wings fluttering,
My friends playing the harp and singing
Underneath the glimmering light of the moon
And the stars
Over Bethlehem I sang.
I told the shepherds, Jesus was coming,
God's representative on Earth.
When he was born, I sang,
I sang my heart out,
The salty breeze whistling past me.
I felt joy when I heard that baby cry,
When I Razpath, an angel of God, saw Jesus.

Briony Stewart (11)
Elmvale Primary School, Annan

Christmas Witness

As I descended from the heavens with my fellow angels
To the small thatched stable in Bethlehem,
I noticed we were the starlight.
I was the guide for travellers coming from far and near.
I had been watching Joseph, Mary and the donkey
Struggling to Bethlehem.
As everyone gathered in the stable, including us angels,
There was a faint smell of mud and grass -
I think coming from the shepherds!
I sensed the kings felt majestic
But not as majestic as He, the One, the King.
I could hear the fluttering of my jewel-encrusted wings,
My robe was the colour of ivory, lined with silver gems.
The night was astonishingly clear for the winter
And Orion watched down.
That is as far as I can remember.
I am God's eyes, His ears and His messenger.
I am Gabriel.
I was there.

Eloise Dunham (10)
Elmvale Primary School, Annan

Christmas Witness

That night, that very special night, I was there.
It was me, the angel.
I saw it all,
I was circling overhead,
As the starlight and the moon shone.
In the hay, the animals watched too.
Then I realised that that was our magnificent gift,
That tiny child,
Just born, one minute ago,
In an old stable in Bethlehem.

Josephine Chan (11)
Elmvale Primary School, Annan

The Angel's Story

I was there.
I saw the big, yellow star twinkling against the dark sky
And the moon shivering as if it was cold.
I saw the shepherds with their sheep
And the three kings stumbling and slouching,
They looked so tired.
I saw the stable and heard the baby crying.
I flew down and there I saw the baby sleeping.
Then came the kings with gold, frankincense and myrrh.
I saw everything at that happy time.
It was me, Gabriel, the angel.

Corrie Mundle (11)
Elmvale Primary School, Annan

Fireworks

Freeze as I light up the sky!
Like the sun in the night,
Gaze as I erupt into sapphire!
Jade!
Rubies and emeralds!
Behold as I blind you with my dazzling colours!
Stand still as I burst out jewels!
Shiver as I terrorise your animals!
Watch my crimson rays shoot around the sky!
Be amazed as I charge into the open!
Clap as my short life ends.
Farewell!

Ricky Addison (11)
Elmvale Primary School, Annan

Christmas Witness

One special, cold, winter night,
I put my gold and silver cloak on.
There was a gigantic star over on the left.
Starlight is so bright.
There in front were three, slow and tired shepherds,
Dropping down onto their knees, starving for food.
I was flying over the city, high and wide,
Singing to Mary, Joseph and Jesus.
I was singing over Bethlehem
As I am an angel.

Rachel Stevenson (11)
Elmvale Primary School, Annan

Colours

Red is like a scented rose with petals growing out.
Yellow is like a little bird flying round and about.
Green is like a field of grass, a grazing ground for sheep.
Blue is like a cloudless sky, with birds all going *cheep, cheep!*
Pink is like a flamingo, standing on one leg.
Orange is like a yummy fruit, sweet to the last dregs.
Purple is like a juicy plum, sitting in the fruit tub.
Brown is like a muddy puddle, down by the nearest pub.
White is like the gentle snow, falling soft and light.
Grey is like a storm cloud, gathering at great height.
Black is like a winter night, with wind howling away.
Gold is like the sun's rays, brightening up the day.
Aqua is like a tropical sea with as many fish as can be.
And there's the rainbow shining up high above a tree
And in the tree are giant peaches, reaching down to me.

Eleanor MacKinnon (11)
Eoligarry Primary School, Northbay

Inside

Little child, little star,
When you're grown you'll go so far,
For now you'll stay in your little room,
But maybe when you're older you'll go to the moon,
Not long to go you will be born soon.

You grow bigger every day,
You feel so comfy you want to stay,
Coming out to a big new world,
Are you a boy or are you a girl?
Will you have straight hair or will you have a curl?

Your mum eats healthy so you'll be strong,
You will be so smart, you'll never be wrong,
Everyone excited, waiting on you,
Anytime you want, just come through,
You very special child.

Here you come, now you're ready, come on,
Now you're grown up and you're so strong,
Coming down like being on a slide,
Wee! You think inside your mind,
We see your head it's coming now.

Out you pop, a beautiful creature,
We just watch the smile on your feature,
Gorgeous child, miracle from Heaven,
When you're two your brother will be seven,
Oh what a joy to have you in our lives.

'It's a boy!' the nurse says sounding very happy,
While she puts on your first ever nappy,
You are so pretty, you'll never be vain,
But wait, what is our name?
I wonder what it is, we'll find out again.

Annemarie MacNeil (10)
Eoligarry Primary School, Northbay

Oh Little Thing

Oh little dormouse
Where do you stay
In a hole in a cornfield
Miles away?

Oh old tree
What is your history? Seeing things born,
Seeing things fall
Won't you tell us it all?

Oh wise elephant
With a memory so long
Won't you trumpet us a song?

Oh green alien
Where do you live?
Where do you stay?
No one knows anything about you
Won't you please say?

All these things are good and great
But my life definitely takes the bait
I live in a warm and cosy house, with TV,
I live with all my family
And they're always there for me
Long, short, big and small
But I love my life most of all.

Christine MacLean (11)
Eoligarry Primary School, Northbay

Midnight Madness

During the night,
I get a fright,
I'm awake for another Midnight Madness, I brush my hair,
And go down the stairs.

In the living room,
There's a witch on her broom,
Out I run to the dining room.

In here I feel happy,
Now as I sit I'm being watched,
So I suddenly turn very snappy,
My spine goes cold,
I go to the kitchen and the phone is still on hold.

I walk in and fall
I slide nearly into the hall,
I feel a toy, I press it hard,
Bananas In Pyjamas it sings,
I hate that song so I go to the hall.

I fall over,
In the hall,
I see a fairy I think,
I do and it stinks,
I go to the toilet, the last room.

I hide in the bath,
Oh no, a spider comes, oh no, it has maths,
The witch and the ghost surround me,
The banana in pyjamas and the fairy sing,
I feel a thump, oh I escaped somehow,
I sleep till another Midnight Madness.

Innes MacDonald (11)
Eoligarry Primary School, Northbay

Fairy Tales

Lots of fairy tales
Lots and lots
Some find them hidden
In a tiny little box
In the cupboard
Dark and fun
Who is singing? Tommy Nun.
Where they live
In a dark purple hole
Singing the good old western stroll.
When you open the book they cook
They look so dark and very scary
Even now they are actually hairy.
Inside they are filled with love and joy
But on the outside they are scary and always annoy.

Kristie Boyd (8)
Eoligarry Primary School, Northbay

Space

Rockets flying, stars whizzing
My juice is really fizzing.
Astronauts floating weightless in the sky
As an alien gives a wave goodbye!

Bouncy, bouncy on the moon
Not like a massive silly goon
No matter how big or small
You won't have a very big fall.

Going round Pluto's orbit
I met an alien called Mr Gorbit!
The planets whizz and the sun goes fizz
Now it's time for a space quiz.

Is Mars made of rock or gases?
Then a big spaceship passes!

Andrew Henderson (11)
Eoligarry Primary School, Northbay

Little Fox In The Box

Little fox in the box
Don't you want to play?
Don't be scared even if you have a beard
I'll laugh anyway.

I love your beard, your nose, your eyes
Gosh, I'm good at telling lies.
I love you when you're above the school,
Chasing a ball in a room.

Little fox in the box
Don't you hide on me
Look outside and see
Don't be bad because you are mad.

Little fox in the box
Why don't you look at me?
Am I nasty or bad
Or mad or sad?

Kayleighanne O'Carroll (8)
Eoligarry Primary School, Northbay

Little Man, Little Man

Little man, little man,
All on your own,
Little man, little man,
Time to go home.

Little man, little man,
In your tiny clothes,
Little man, little man,
With your tiny nose.

Little man, little man,
Time to go to bed,
Little man, little man,
Rest your sleepy head.

Aileen Elder (11)
Eoligarry Primary School, Northbay

The Shore

Down the shore
It is cold
When your fingers touch the icy water
It's like a dentist's jaw.
You can see fishermen passing
When you're fishing for winkles
Reaching into the cracks and crevices
You might see a crab
Watch out, it might pinch you
If you find a cracked cockle
You can kick it off to Mars.
If you're bored
Go over to the rocks
Find a feather
Dip it in water
And write on a stone
And pretend to be Thomas Jefferson.

Ryan MacNeil (10)
Eoligarry Primary School, Northbay

Casper The Ghost

Casper was a friendly ghost
Who went to Mars
To buy some cars

Casper was a nasty ghost
Who likes to bully others
But we say he is bad

Casper was a clever ghost
Who went to college
To get more knowledge

Casper was a thin ghost
Who never ate a lot
Because he left his food to rot.

Jordon MacNeil (9)
Eoligarry Primary School, Northbay

Haunted House

In a haunted house,
Lived a granny and a mouse,
The granny wore a blouse
And drank Famous Grouse.

We could see ghouls,
Sitting on stools,
We could hear Frankenstein's whines,
It sent chills down our spines.

We could see the troll called Mr Rolling,
He could play fiddle, football and bowling,
Seeing the dragon called Brock,
Gave us a nasty shock.

Look, there's a goblin running around,
Wow! Did you see that witch fall to the ground?
Look, another witch,
Playing on a football pitch.

There's Nessie,
She's looking a bit messy.
There's King Kong,
Whacking his gong.

Micheal Mackinnon (9)
Eoligarry Primary School, Northbay

The Woolly Mammoth

The woolly mammoth's head
Is bigger than . . .
My teacher
He is very, very woolly!
Woollier than . . .
My jumper
His tusks are bigger than . . .
Me!

Gemma Stables (8)
Fetterangus Primary School, Peterhead

Stop The War

Bang! Bang!
The war has started
Bang! Bang!
Everybody is dying
Bang! Bang!
Fight for your country
Bang! Bang!
Your country depends on you
Bang!

Grant Stephen (11)
Fetterangus Primary School, Peterhead

Aliens

I have a pet alien
His name is Gazalien.

He came in a rocket
That could fit in my pocket.

He used to eat lots of feet
But now he eats lots of meat.

Now he has grown so big
He's the size of an oil rig.

Daniel Lewczenko (9)
Fetterangus Primary School, Peterhead

Clownfish

Clownfish are colourful
They swim very quickly
They eat lots of fish flakes
For their snacks and lunch
They are always willing to munch!

Laura Whyte (11)
Fetterangus Primary School, Peterhead

The Silver River

There is a place far, far away
With a unicorn that plays all day.
'Let's go and play at the river
The river that is silver.'

'Have a drink of the river . . . '
'Stop!' says a creature called Snowdrop.
'My friend once drank it and passed away
You don't want that to happen today.'

'That's very sad that the river is polluted
And very bad that people do it.'
Off they go and play together,
All day long forever and ever.

Chelsea Osler (9)
Fetterangus Primary School, Peterhead

Roller Coaster Ride

Roller coasters do loop-the-loop
Roller coasters go up, up, up
And then down, down, down,
Left and right,
Up and down
But my favourite part is going really fast!

Jordan Osler (7)
Fetterangus Primary School, Peterhead

Smoking Is A Bad Influence

Smoking is a bad influence
It makes your clothes stink
You get yellow teeth, black lungs
And bad breath -
Smoking kills!

William Lunan (11)
Fetterangus Primary School, Peterhead

All About The World

The sky is blue
Houses are grey, brown and black
The ground is green and brown
Animals are brown, grey, green
Orange, yellow, purple and white
The sun comes out when it is day
The moon comes out when it is night
The mountains are white, purple and brown
The world is shaped like a sphere
Fields are green and brown
The sea is blue.

Ewan Ritchie (8)
Fetterangus Primary School, Peterhead

Jack-In-The-Box

I can jump and scream
I am funny and scary too
I am happy to surprise you!

I'm a jack-in-the-box
It is dark
I am scared
I am waiting to be opened
So I can startle you!

Sophie Will (8)
Fetterangus Primary School, Peterhead

Snowflakes

Snowflakes shine through the air
They are so light
And bright
They are white
They are white in the light.

Alex Ewart (7)
Fetterangus Primary School, Peterhead

The Girl Who Smacked Into A Door

There was a girl from P4
Who smacked into a door
She had a headache
And made an earthquake
And she wasn't seen anymore.

Rebecca Armstrong-Haimes (8)
Fishermoss School, Portlethen

I'm Eleven

There was a young boy in P7
He wanted to see inside Heaven
So he started to hit
Then had a bad fit
And said, 'It's because I'm eleven.'

Brook McKimmie (11)
Fishermoss School, Portlethen

Dizziness

There was a young man from P4
Who knocked himself out on the floor
He screamed and he shouted
Till everything was mounted
And knocked his head off the door.

Rachel McPherson (11)
Fishermoss School, Portlethen

A Boy In P4

There was a young man in P4
He walked straight into a school door
Then he rubbed his head
And fell into bed
Then he lay down and thumped on the floor.

Struan McLennan (8)
Fishermoss School, Portlethen

Eleven

There was a girl in P7
Who thought that she'd go to Heaven
She dreamt every day
And always would say,
'I'll never be as old as eleven!'

Beth Trotter (11)
Fishermoss School, Portlethen

The King And Ling

There once was a lady called Ling
Who wanted to marry a king
So she went to the palace
That was located in Dallas
And then they got married in spring.

Emma Petrie (11)
Fishermoss School, Portlethen

The Silly Girl

There was a young girl from P4
She walked straight into a door
She fell on her bum
And sucked her thumb
And that was the girl from P4.

Caitlyn Webster (8)
Fishermoss School, Portlethen

Dan Is The Man

There was a boy called Dan
He lived in a caravan
Once it caught fire
It crushed his desire
And all that was left was a can.

Scott Harper (11)
Fishermoss School, Portlethen

Dennis Strikes Again

Once there was a boy who played tennis
His name was Dennis
He played it every day
He won it on sports day
And everyone thought he was a menace.

Jordan Pattinson (8)
Fishermoss School, Portlethen

The Nutty Professor

There once was a man aged forty
Who built a robot called Cortly
Some people say he was a nutty professor
And then he fell down a compressor
And his last words were, 'I expect I'll be seeing you shortly.'

Duncan Barclay (11)
Fishermoss School, Portlethen

The Young Girl

There was a young girl in P4
Who slipped and fell on the floor
She had blood on her shirt
Her jaw really hurt
And she was really, really sore.

Chelsea McIntyre (8)
Fishermoss School, Portlethen

The Zit

There once was a young boy called Kit
On his bottom there was a large zit
He dabbed it with oil
It turned into a boil
And now he's unable to sit!

Cameron Bradford (9)
Fishermoss School, Portlethen

The Footballer From Nepal

There was a young man from Nepal
Whose favourite sport was football
He dribbled and dived
And played 5 a-side
But he couldn't score a goal at all.

Gary Darnell (11)
Fishermoss School, Portlethen

Circus Clown

I want to be a circus clown
Jump about and fool around
I'd love to run and play all day
And not be told what to say
I'd love to be a circus clown
And never have to wear a frown.

Grace Hardie (11)
Fishermoss School, Portlethen

The Boy From P7

There was a young boy in P7
Who was from little Devon
His tummy started to rumble
The world started to crumble
Stupid old boy from P7.

Jordan Rae (11)
Fishermoss School, Portlethen

Birthday Boy

There was once a young boy in P7
Who had just turned eleven
He got a new pen
After he was glad he wasn't ten
But remembered he was travelling to Devon.

Martyn Black (11)
Fishermoss School, Portlethen

The Young Man From Aberdeen

There was a young man from Aberdeen
He always wanted to clean
His name was Bob
And he didn't do his job
Then he went to lunch with the Queen.

Ross McMurray (11)
Fishermoss School, Portlethen

Kevin

There once was a boy called Kevin
Who thought it was ten past seven
He couldn't see the time
But heard the clock chime
Then knew it was half-past eleven.

Andrew Thomson (11)
Fishermoss School, Portlethen

Mars

There was a young boy from Mars
Who liked to eat lots of Mars bars
He liked them so much
Then he heard a big crunch
Then he grew lots of scars.

Kirsty Munro (9)
Fishermoss School, Portlethen

The Bumpful Butterfly

There was a young butterfly
Who always liked to try
To show off her wings
And fly round in rings
Until she bumped her wing and started to cry.

Siân Robertson (8)
Fishermoss School, Portlethen

Smelly Jelly

My mum made some jelly
And it was very, very smelly
It sticks in my throat
And I begin to choke
And it still lies in my belly.

Natalie Begg (9)
Fishermoss School, Portlethen

Dolly The Dolphin

There was a dolphin called Dolly
Who loved to use her brolly
It opened and closed
Then bashed her on the nose
She cried then got a fish lolly.

Nicola Yeats (11)
Fishermoss School, Portlethen

Sick?

There was a young boy in P7
Who was going to be eleven
He nearly felt sick
Felt like a brick
And wanted to go to Heaven.

Natesh Shivakumar (11)
Fishermoss School, Portlethen

Shiver River

There was a young man from Aberdeen
Who wanted to swim in the river Dee
He got in the river
And had a shiver
And met a new friend called Lee.

Nathan Sussex (11)
Fishermoss School, Portlethen

Floors And Doors

There was once a girl in P4
Who loved to go through the door
She ate some ice cream
Then had a big dream
That she was stuck under the floor.

Mrithula Shivakumar (8)
Fishermoss School, Portlethen

Bike Man

There once was a man on a bike
Who felt he was riding a trike
He lost a wheel
And did a deal
Then he started to hike.

Craig Archibald (11)
Fishermoss School, Portlethen

A Girl Called Cassey

There was once a young girl called Cassey
Who had a dog called Masey
The dog got lost
And got found in the moss
And the dog was really messy.

Kelsie Kidd (11)
Fishermoss School, Portlethen

A New Toy Got Broken

There was once a wee boy
Who broke his new toy
He went to his mum
I want a new toy
But he didn't get a new toy.

Casie Greig (8)
Fishermoss School, Portlethen

The Gym Teacher

There was a gym teacher at school
Who I thought was really cool
In the end
She started to bend
And then she snapped in two.

Matthew Hancock (11)
Fishermoss School, Portlethen

The Mouse

There once was a mouse called Fred
He lived in the garden shed
One day he went outside
He was sent to find the rat
Called Ted.

Kieran Leith (8)
Fishermoss School, Portlethen

Spidy Hike

There once was a spider called Spike
Who liked playing on his bike
He cycled through the dark
And even through the park
But really liked going for a hike.

Ross Gordon (8)
Fishermoss School, Portlethen

The Rain

The rain is like tears
Dripping from the sky
The rain is like hammers
When it hits the ground
The rain is a glittering, twinkling thing
From the snow-white clouds
When wind blows rain it slaps and whips
The rain gushes everywhere
But people are inside.

Amy Bagshaw (7)
Flora Stevenson Primary School, Edinburgh

Rain

The rain is like a hammer battering and pounding
It is like tears dripping from a sad face
It is like pearls falling from the sky
The rain is like snowflakes swaying from the clouds
The rain is like stars.

Jenny Grant (7)
Flora Stevenson Primary School, Edinburgh

My Papa

My papa is oh so sweet,
He often will buy me a treat.

He taught me how to play chess
And now gets himself in a bit of a mess!

He is a very happy chap
And nowadays needs an afternoon nap.

He used to be quite fat,
But has now slimmed down as a matter of fact.

Health for him is not so good,
I wish I could help him more if I could.

Although he is the age of 73,
I sometimes think he acts the same age as me!

I love my papa, yes I do
And I know he loves me, the same way too.

David Hand (9)
Flora Stevenson Primary School, Edinburgh

The Jungle

The jungle is a wet, wet place,
Rain comes down and soaks your face.

Animals lurk everywhere,
So watch your step and take great care.

You pitch a tent, you light a fire,
Warm yourself and make you drier.

The day comes and mosquitoes bite,
Lots of blood for their delight.

The jungle is a scary place,
You want to go home, you want to race!

Sam Riley (9)
Flora Stevenson Primary School, Edinburgh

Rain

The rain is like diamonds falling out of the clouds
It is like pearls growing in the sea
It is like stars glittering in the night sky
The rain is like tears falling from a sad face.

Rachael Addison (7)
Flora Stevenson Primary School, Edinburgh

The Tree

Huge brown trunk
Rough and cracked
Like a wooden body
Long branches like arms
And little twigs like fingers.

Many trees have magical leaves
They change into yellow in spring
They change into green in summer
They change into red in the autumn
And leaves fall to the ground in winter.

A tree has many friends
Birds and squirrels
Birds sing for the tree
Squirrels play in the tree.

Oh what a happy tree!

Hansol Moon (10)
Flora Stevenson Primary School, Edinburgh

What Raindrops Remind Me Of

Raindrops remind me of crystals.
Rain is like silver stars glistening in the night sky.
Rain is like a banging drum never to stop.
Rain reminds me of snowdrops opening.

Emma Wright (7)
Flora Stevenson Primary School, Edinburgh

Summer Holidays

H omesick sometimes you get,
O n a boat, slipping upon the deck.
L ying on the beach in the sun,
I n comes the tide ruining your fun.
D ays on end looking at the rain
A nd you fall asleep dreaming of fame.
Y awning after the sleep you had,
S uddenly you feel like screaming like mad.

Tommy Loan (10)
Flora Stevenson Primary School, Edinburgh

Red

Dragon breathes hot fire,
Sunset
Looks like it's going to be sunny,
Roses smell like perfume.

Emma Rattray (7)
Fossoway Primary School, Kinross

Black

A dark, spooky graveyard
Near a big old church
A spider on a web
A bat comes and
Swoops over the dead bodies,
Under the ground.

George Logan (7)
Fossoway Primary School, Kinross

The Moon

The moon glows like a flickering candle in a small dark room.
Beams like a torch shining on a pitch-black night.
Glitters like water in the dark, lit up by starlight.
Shimmers like fireworks exploding in the sky on a gloomy night
Moves like a kite gliding through the cloudy sky.

Callum Fare (10)
Fossoway Primary School, Kinross

The Moon

The moon glows like a Hallowe'en lantern carried
around the pitch-black streets.
Stares like a cat peering down on the shadowy town on a misty night.
Gleams like a shiny disco ball lighting up a murky old dance floor.
Moves like a mouse scampering silently across the muddy, wet lawn.
Shines like a lamp with a brilliant white bulb in a dark bedroom.
Glistens like a snail leaving its slimy, silvery trail
in the snowy white garden.

Callum Mullen (9)
Fossoway Primary School, Kinross

The Moon

The moon glitters like a huge round disco ball
twirling at a musical party.
Shimmers like a show of fireworks in the dark sky
with colourful splashes.
Sparkles like a bright fire burning on a Bonfire Night
with sparks bursting out of the fire.
Twinkles like the bright yellow stars
in the midnight sky on a quiet night.
Dazzles like a bright, gleaming torch shining
on the pathway on a dark, misty night.

Katy Johnson (8)
Fossoway Primary School, Kinross

The Moon

The moon shines like a gleaming crystal glass in a posh restaurant.
Beams like a bright torch in a pitch-black forest.
Glows like a pumpkin lantern on a dark Hallowe'en.
Prances like a graceful dancer in a beautiful silk dress.
Gleams like a fluorescent jacket in the thick swirling fog.
Sparkles like a glittering disco outfit in a big wardrobe.

Jane Somervail (10)
Fossoway Primary School, Kinross

The Moon

The moon shimmers like a glistening disco ball that sparkles
at a Hallowe'en party.
Glows like an orange lava lamp in the darkness of my room.
Glitters like sparks from fireworks exploding across the pitch-black sky.

Rachel Hepburn (9)
Fossoway Primary School, Kinross

The Moon

The moon shines like a torch in pitch-black night
Carried through the scary woods at Hallowe'en.
Glows like a cat's eyes on a dark night strolling through a black park.
Beams like a red laser beam touching the other side of the room.
Dazzles like a star in the sky on Christmas Eve
above the stable in Bethlehem.
Drifts like an elegant swan swimming across a light blue pond.

Laura Cheyne
Fossoway Primary School, Kinross

The Moon

The moon sparkles like a beautiful diamond on my engagement ring
that lights up a room in the dark.
Dazzles like a bright lamp in the night beaming to keep the room alight.
Drifts like a swan sailing across the crystal clear lake.
Beams like fireworks twirling in the sky lighting up a town
on Bonfire Night.
Dances like an elegant ballerina twirling around a dim stage.

Nicole Emslie (10)
Fossoway Primary School, Kinross

The Moon

The moon dazzles like a bright torch light
shining heavily with no switch off button.
Stares like a spy on a secret mission
running through the dark, wet street.
Moves like a hawk gliding fiercely through the sky at night,
lost in the blackness.
Beams like a powerful bright street light on the dark pavement.

Calum Greer (10)
Fossoway Primary School, Kinross

The Moon

The moon prances like a ballroom dancer on a black dance floor.
Shines like a bedside lamp in a darkened room.
Sparkles like a guiser in his glittering costume.
Shimmers like broken glass on a damp, wet path
through a dark garden.
Floats like a buzzard over its prey on a misty morning.

Kieran Carruthers (10)
Fossoway Primary School, Kinross

The Moon

The moon shines like a Hallowe'en lantern
with a huge scary face on a spooky night.
Sparkles like a beady eye of a cat sitting on a wall,
on a cold winter's evening.
Beams like traffic lights helping drivers
through the thick mist on the narrow, dark road.
Glows like a glow-worm in a deep, dull cave,
gleaming against the roof.

Ben Cooper (9)
Fossoway Primary School, Kinross

The Moon

The moon glistens like a huge disco ball with all the stars
dancing round.
Drifts like a swan swimming across the ripples on the water
from the midnight breeze.
Beams like a lamp post giving light to everyone in its path.
Glitters like pieces of magic dust falling from the sky,
giving everything a touch of silver.

Ellie Scott-Gray (9)
Fossoway Primary School, Kinross

The Moon

The moon drifts like an eagle soaring over the high mountain peak.
Like a silvery white swan floating on a crystal darkness.
Like a log drifting on the black rippling water.
Like a shimmering fish at the very bottom of the deep ocean floor.

Calum Hutchison (9)
Fossoway Primary School, Kinross

I Wish, I Wish, I Wish

I wish I could have a load of money,
so I can buy some honey.
I wish I could own a successful games company,
so I could have all of the top game names.
I wish I could have my own private cruiser,
so I would no longer be a loser.
I wish that I could teleport,
so that I wouldn't have to run around town.
I wish I was immortal,
at all those dead people I would chortle.

Philip Allan (11)
Foulford Primary School, Cowdenbeath

My Wish Poem

I wish I had a jet pack so I could fly high in the sky,
I wish I had a million pounds so I could buy anything,
I wish I could stop time so I could do anything I wanted,
I wish I had a jet so I wouldn't get wet,
I wish I could go swimming whenever I wanted,
I wish I could have chocolate but not a lot,
I wish, I wish, I wish, I wish.

Scott Aitken (11)
Foulford Primary School, Cowdenbeath

My Poem

I wish I had a quad bike so I can zoom anywhere.
I wish I had a Hummer limousine so I can relax.
I wish I had a football pitch so I can play football all the time.
I wish I had a jet so I can go places fast.
I wish I had a mansion so I have lots of room.

Kieran Pierce (11)
Foulford Primary School, Cowdenbeath

My Five Wishes

If I had five wishes I'd wish for a mansion
That was 40 storeys high
Have a maid, room service and an excellent chef
Who'd make cookies, cakes and apple crumble pie.

A theme park outside
That was always jam-packed
It would be so cool and fun
That people who were serious, would stay until they cracked.

Owning Hollywood
That's filled with movie stars
I'd star, create and direct
The new programme on TV that's called 'Life on Mars'.

I'd own a lot of sports cars
That are fast and furious
I'd have tinted windows
Leaving everyone curious.

I'd definitely own
A successful gem mine
That would run right under
The famous river Tyne.

Ross McArthur (11)
Foulford Primary School, Cowdenbeath

I Wish

So I wish to be famous and rich
To count all my coins, gold and silver
I wish for all the PS2 games,
So I could play other things old and new
I wish for all the chocolate milk
So I could drink until my heart's content
I wish there was no school,
So the work isn't cruel
I wish I could be an artist
So my work now doesn't drool.

Robert Candlish (11)
Foulford Primary School, Cowdenbeath

A Wish Poem

Rangers, Rangers, I would play,
So I could score goals every day.

I wish from a drum kit
So I could play, play and play every day.

I wish for a jet so I could fly
Up high in the sky
And I could fly for free on fly be,

I wish for a big house
So I could run, run, run, run and have some fun.

I wish for some money, loads if you can
I'll spend it well on a car or even a van.

Connor Balfour (11)
Foulford Primary School, Cowdenbeath

I Wish, I Wish, I Wish

I wish for a lifetime supply of chocolate
So I can eat when I want.

I wish to have a private island
So I can go whenever I want.

I wish, I wish, I wish.

I wish to have a private plane
So I can go to my island.

I wish I had a Subaru Impretza
With gold rims and blue body.

I wish to be king
So I can live in a castle.

Fraser Thomson (11)
Foulford Primary School, Cowdenbeath

I Wish, I Wish, I Wish

I wish I had a jet,
So I can catch clouds in a fishing net.

I wish I had £1,000,000,000,
So I could have a party and make lots of sound.

I wish I had a PSP
So I could play games and eat my tea.

I wish I had a Ferrari
And zoom past everyone on the motorway.

I wish I could play for Rangers
And play in front of strangers.

James Jack (11)
Foulford Primary School, Cowdenbeath

I Wish

I wish I could go to Australia
To see my best friend Briony.

I wish I could swim with dolphins
To see them jump out of the water.

I wish to see Rangers play at Ibrox
It would be a dream come true.

I wish to see dolphins at sea
To see them jumping and twirling out of the water.

I wish, I wish, I wish.

Meghan Roy (11)
Foulford Primary School, Cowdenbeath

I Wish

I wish my family could live forever
Because they are the best.

And a lifetime supply of money
So I could spend it so wisely.

So then I could meet the Rangers players
To meet them and say thanks.

I wish I could have a snooker table
Because it is the best of games.

And a lifetime supply of sweets
So I could eat them every day.

Kerrie McLeod (11)
Foulford Primary School, Cowdenbeath

My Poem

I wish I could be a black belt in karate
So I can instruct.

I wish I had a lifetime supply of chocolate
So I can eat when I want.

I wish I had a big quad bike
So I can zoom anywhere.

I wish I could have a healthy life
So I could always be fit.

I wish I could wish whenever I want
So I could have everything.

Jack Sneddon (11)
Foulford Primary School, Cowdenbeath

My Wish

I wish I had a mansion
A big house would be great.
I wish I were the President
Of the United States.
I wish I had Ibrox Stadium
I'd have room to play football.
I wish I had a PSP
I could play it anywhere at all.
I wish I was in the year 3000
I could try new things.
I wish I had a camper van
In the morning I could hear the birds sing.

Keir Shepherd (11)
Foulford Primary School, Cowdenbeath

My Dream Wish

I wish, I wish I could be rich
With a bright, shiny, red sports car.
Everyone would be jealous and want a shot.
I wish I could own a three-storey mansion with a swimming pool
I could laze around all day and swim.

I wish I could go in a limousine
With Kelly Clarkson and Britney and Jamie Lynn
Because I like them and it would be nice to meet someone that is cool.

Nicole Logan (11)
Foulford Primary School, Cowdenbeath

I Wish

I wish I had ten million pounds,
To spend on what I wish.
I wish for a large house with huge gardens,
For more freedom, space and room.
I wish I could own a private island,
To live on at my leisure.
I wish I had a parrot, a monkey and three dogs,
I would play with them, I'd love them and they would love me back.

I wish I could sit down and write a book
Because I never can.
I wish I could meet Enid Blyton characters,
They would be so interesting.
I wish I could have all this, but then again
I could settle for a box of Mars Delights instead!

William Brown (11)
Foulford Primary School, Cowdenbeath

I Wish

I wish for a massive mansion, so I could have lots of rooms
to play my games in.
I wish to be able to fly, to see everything from up high.
I wish to have a huge silver limousine because it would be comfortable.
I wish to have a big theme park, so I could have lots of money.
I wish for a bowling alley with lots of lanes to play on
and spend the whole day in it.

Ross Barclay (10)
Foulford Primary School, Cowdenbeath

My Five Wishes

I wish I was immortal
So I could not die.

I wish I had a jet pack
So that I could fly so high.

I wish I had a sports car
That goes 500mph.

I wish I was an outlaw
That steals and breaks the law.

I wish I was an artist
So I can paint and draw.

Bobby Robson (11)
Foulford Primary School, Cowdenbeath

Being A Kid Is Great

Being a kid is great,
The only things that annoy me are,
My bossy parents,
They sometimes make me eat Brussels sprouts
And things that I do not like.

But apart from that I love my life,
My parents normally buy me stuff,
I might not like doing chores
But I would do everything for money,
They gave me what I wanted most for my birthday last year.

I like going swimming and my parents let me go to clubs,
I made my dad a valentine's card
He gave me a hug and a kiss and said, 'Thank you!'
I love my parents they are the best.
Being a kid is *great!*

Ellen Brabender (8)
Garelochhead Primary School, Garelochhead

Me And My Mum

Me and my mum cook,
Me and my mum read a book.
Sometimes we fight,
But then we make up.
She goes to work at 9am
Then she comes home at 5pm.

My mum is very nice,
But sometimes she can be very bossy.
She buys me nice clothes,
But some are not very nice.
Sometimes I am very cheeky,
Then it makes her angry.

She lets me go to parties,
She lets me go to bed at half nine,
But at weekends she lets me go later
At whatever time I want.
I love my mum very much.

Stephanie Niven (9)
Garelochhead Primary School, Garelochhead

What I Do On A Monday

On a Monday I get up and get dressed,
Get my breakfast and all the rest,
Walk to school all by myself,
Wait in line for the bell to ring,
Do all the work that's on the board,
Go home and do my homework,
After that I will play with my friends,
Then go in and have my tea,
Watch the telly at six o'clock,
At seven o'clock I will have a bath,
After that I will get some milk and cookies,
Then go to bed and hope I have a nice dream.

Siobhan McKay (8)
Garelochhead Primary School, Garelochhead

Summer And Winter

In the summer I go to my nana's,
In the summer I go to my aunt's,
It is fun in the summer.
I get to play on my bike and roller skates,
In the summer I never get grounded,
In the summer it is the best for me
Everyone plays out and no one goes in.

The winter is so much fun for me,
I get to play in the snow,
I make fat, round, white snowmen
With all my friends and family.
The snow and the rain I love them both
The snow and the rain they're just the best.
The summer and the winter I love them.

Adrianne Jones (8)
Garelochhead Primary School, Garelochhead

Young And Wild Animals

When animals are just born everyone thinks
They might get injured or killed.
But I think that it is
The best days of their lives.

A baby is vulnerable
But playful, cute and cuddly too.
The squeak of a baby lion, the chirp of a baby bird,
The squeal of a baby meerkat.

All these baby animals
Are part of this world.
So take care of them,
They won't last forever.

Isla Monaghan (9)
Garelochhead Primary School, Garelochhead

My Dalmatian Puppy

My dogs always played with my dog called Tilly.
My Dalmatians were called Ollie and Oscar
They were so funny.

Ollie always whined,
Oscar always barked
And Tilly always jumped
Into the bath with Oscar.

When we were moving
They had to go to someone else.
When they went into the car,
Ollie jumped into the front seat.

Olivia Handforth (8)
Garelochhead Primary School, Garelochhead

Things I Like To Do

I like to watch television,
I like to build with my Lego.
I enjoy playing with my dog,
I play games with my kitten,
Running around in gym class is fun.

Jake Quigley (8)
Garelochhead Primary School, Garelochhead

My Parents

My parents are nice but when I am bad I get grounded
And I am not allowed out and it is boring
But all my friends are allowed out
The next day is when I am allowed out,
My friends come in my house
And we play the PlayStation.

George Skea (8)
Garelochhead Primary School, Garelochhead

My Mum Baked A Cake

Last night my mum made a cake,
My other brother helped her.
After she made the cake she baked it in the oven,
It said two hours exactly.

Then after two hours she forgot
She got a phone call saying, 'Mum come pick me up.'
My two sisters called
When she came home the phone went off in the garden.

My brother called, he wanted a lift home as well.
So she did not get into the house.
When she came home with my two brothers
And my two sisters, that cake she made was baked all right!
When we brought it out of the oven, it was black.
The house was black, I was coughing
And I could not see, it was like a fire.

Alana Dick (9)
Garelochhead Primary School, Garelochhead

Roses

Roses, roses everywhere,
Everywhere I look
The smell of roses is like Heaven in the air,
Oh roses, my breath you took.
Roses, roses, without you what would I be?
Never fall apart
You are always beside me.
Roses, roses, you are close to my heart
Roses, roses, when you die
How will I cope?
When you die I never lie,
Because you are my only hope,
I see you in the river,
The river is where your petals float.

Rebekka Lamont (10)
Gartcosh Primary School, Gartcosh

A Mythical World

Somewhere that nobody goes,
Only mythical creatures know,
It's filled with laughter and joy
Only goblins will tempt to annoy,
There's fairies and goblins and lots more too
Every day there's loads to do,
There's troll towers and fairy falls,
At seven o'clock the pixie calls,
The leprechaun brings you loads of luck,
The dragons sometimes play in the muck,
The unicorn flies with its spiky horn,
In the water, mermaids are born,
Hopefully these creatures won't be forgot,
'Cause there are so many, in fact, there's a lot!

Alannah Graham (9)
Gartcosh Primary School, Gartcosh

Games, Games

Games, games are just my thing,
The more I play, the more I'm laughing,
As I play every day
I sing and dance in any way.

Games, games are the best,
I like to play with the rest,
Netball, football, basketball too,
I can't choose which one to do.

Games, games are lots of fun,
Just the thing for everyone,
Some of my games weigh a ton
While I play, oh I have so much fun!

Toni Robertson (9)
Gartcosh Primary School, Gartcosh

Football

I like football,
It's so much fun.
Football, football,
A game for everyone.
I like football,
Even though I don't feel like running,
Football, football,
But the sun is still burning.
I like football,
It's so much fun,
Football, football,
A game for everyone.

Sarah Jarvie
Gartcosh Primary School, Gartcosh

Football Mad

I like football,
It's so much fun.
I can run and run and run.

I like football,
It's a wonderful thing,
It almost makes me want to sing.

I like football,
All the time I like football
It is so fine.

Barry McGuigan (10)
Gartcosh Primary School, Gartcosh

Winston

Winston you are a lovely cat,
But Winston you are very, very fat,
As you swish your tail,
Along the rail,
Sing us your song
And we'll sing along,
Don't be scared,
You will be heard,
Winston when in your bed,
You think school is boring in your head,
Winston, Winston, in Gartcosh School
Winston, Winston, you always rule.

Dawn Abate (10)
Gartcosh Primary School, Gartcosh

Werewolves

Werewolves at night
Wolves at day
Come out now or I will say, 'Hocus pocus go away!'

Werewolves at night
Wolves at day
They come out to play when the moon is shining away.

Werewolves at night
Wolves at day
I'll see you again so hip, hip, hooray.

When the sun is coming they all run away
So bye again, let's make a den.

James Ford (10)
Gartcosh Primary School, Gartcosh

The Great Gorilla

The great greedy gorilla
Grabbed the grey gifted gosling,
Giggling, growling, groaning.

The great, grand, greedy gorilla,
Gave gifts to the gosling,
Generously, gently, grandly.

The great, grand, gross, greedy gorilla,
Played galloping gymnast games with the gosling,
Gracefully, giggling, gallantly.

The great, grand, gross, greedy, groaning gorilla,
Showed off his gifted grand skills to the gosling,
Gratefully, geniusly, grandly.

Callum Galloway (9)
Gartcosh Primary School, Gartcosh

Football

I like football, it's fun
It makes me want to run and run.
I like darts, it takes skill
I like playing darts with my uncle Bill.
Now let's get to my food, it's more than a dream
When my mum cooks, her head has steam.
I like bread, my brother is a nerd,
My uncle does the tombola, I like Coca-Cola.
I have got school bags my sister dresses in rags.
I like music, like rap, I play my big sister at Snap.
In school I have got a task,
In wrestling they wear a mask.

Robert McLean (10)
Gartcosh Primary School, Gartcosh

The Mad House

My aunt's dog is very funny,
It jumps about like a mad bunny.

My uncle is very lazy,
He looks like a hairy canary.
My uncle is so lazy,
He was in his bed till 9 o'clock
And always late for work
That's my uncle.

My aunt does everything in the house
And no one helps her.
When they are in their beds,
She makes their breakfast.
All the house is so lazy,
My aunt goes so crazy
And that's the mad house.

Darren Telfer (8)
Glenlee Primary School, Burnbank

Family Feelings

Mum is happy sometimes
Dad is grumpy sometimes
Brothers are very stupid
Sisters are so sweet.

Gran buys too many sweets
Papa likes to work
Cousins are so loving
Aunts and uncles are the same.

I am happy in every way
People have other families but . . .
This is just mine.

Emma Harper (9)
Glenlee Primary School, Burnbank

My Crazy Pets

My dog is so crazy
My budgie's just daft
My rat's in the bath
My snake's a psychopath
My fish is in the loo
My mum is gonna blow a fuse
My bathroom's like a swimming pool
My brother was acting the fool
My parrot escaped from its cage
And it got the mouse in its mouth
And that was the end of that stupid old mouse.

Calvin Bailey (8)
Glenlee Primary School, Burnbank

Family Feelings

Families live, families die,
Families laugh and families cry!
Families tell the truth and families lie,
Families get along, but not all the time!
But family get-togethers
Are always the best
From the east to the west.

Rhianne Scott (8)
Glenlee Primary School, Burnbank

Red

Red is like a ruby gleaming in the sun.
Red is like blood streaming through my veins.
Red is like lava pouring out of a volcano.
Red is like jelly wobbling on a plate.
Red is like fire burning in the forest.
Red is like the sun shining on the sand.
Red is like grapes, juicy and ready to eat.

Andrew O'Neill (11)
Greenhills Primary School, East Kilbride

Red

Red is for strawberries covered in vanilla ice cream.
Red is like lava shooting from a volcano.
Red is jelly wobbling on a plate.
Red is like grapes which I like to eat.
Red is like fire burning in my fireplace.
Red is my car shining in the sun.
Red is for apples being picked from a tree.
Red is like lipstick which my mum likes to wear.
Red is my face when I'm embarrassed.

Gary Burrell (10)
Greenhills Primary School, East Kilbride

Red

Red is a strawberry that I like to dip in sugar.
Red is a ruby that sparkles in my mum's ring.
Red is a jelly that wobbles in my tummy.
Red is lava boiling in a volcano.
Red is for apples, healthy and delicious.
Red is the brick my house is built with.
Red is a milkshake, nice and thick.
Red is a colour, my favourite one.

Sean Quigley (11)
Greenhills Primary School, East Kilbride

Red

Red is like jelly, nice and wobbly.
Red is like lava, hot and fiery.
Red is like roses ready to pick in the summer.
Red is like lipstick that my aunt wears at parties.
Red is apples, beautiful and juicy.
Red is like fire, hot and burning.
Red is strawberries ready to pick and eat.
Red is a ruby that shines in my ring.

Lana Southworth (11)
Greenhills Primary School, East Kilbride

Blue

Blue is the sky, clear and bright
Blue is like my school jumper I wear every day
Blue is Rangers scoring all night
Blue is like a sapphire glowing on my finger
Blue is for bluebells blowing in the breeze
Blue are my eyes staring at the world
Blue is like a freezing cold Slush Puppy I hate to drink
Blue is my wallpaper, lovely and bright
Blue is my teacher's chair she loves to sit on.

Darrian Darlow (11)
Greenhills Primary School, East Kilbride

Red

Red is a juicy apple, shiny and ready to eat.
Red is fire, very bright and smoky.
Red is strawberries ready to be picked.
Red is a ruby, shining in my gold ring.
Red is the sun, bright on a summer's day.
Red is lava spewing out from a volcano.
Red is a bus stopping for you.
Red is an anger bubble that suddenly goes *pop!*

Morgan Frier (10)
Greenhills Primary School, East Kilbride

Yellow

Yellow are the healthy bananas that I love to eat.
Yellow is the burning sun that brightens up the day.
Yellow are the daffodils that grow in the fields.
Yellow is the colour of a pencil to make a lovely picture.
Yellow is a gold ring that I am wearing just now.
Yellow is a juicy melon, fresh and ready to eat.
Yellow is a roaring lion that you should stay away from.
Yellow is a bright colour that is one of my favourites.

Jacqueline McGinniss (10)
Greenhills Primary School, East Kilbride

Blue

Blue is the sky on a warm summer's day.
Blue is my school jumper, very warm and woolly.
Blue are the bluebells that grow in my garden.
Blue is the sea, crashing on the beach.
Blue is the sapphire on my gold necklace.
Blue are the blueberries growing in the forest.
Blue is my power bus driving down the road.
Blue is the colour of my eyes I use to see the world.
Blue is the teacher's chair
I'd love to see her fall off!

Amanda-Jane Little (10)
Greenhills Primary School, East Kilbride

Blue

Blue is the sky, clear on a sunny day.
Blue is the ocean swaying.
Blue are the bluebells, beautiful in the garden.
Blue are the blueberries freshly picked and ripe to eat.
Blue is the aquamarine in my mum's beautiful ring.
Blue are the Slush Puppies I love to drink.
Blue is my lovely warm jacket that I'm wearing tonight.

Sarah Rose (10)
Greenhills Primary School, East Kilbride

Red

Red is like grapes, juicy and sweet in my mouth.
Red is like lava, hot and fiery.
Red is like the stop sign on the traffic lights.
Red is like a strawberry, squishy and soft.
Red is like a rose blooming in the sun.
Red is like lipstick like my teacher wears every day.
Red is like a robin redbreast that is so dark it is hard to see.
Red is like a ruby on my mum's watch.

Craig Cameron (11)
Greenhills Primary School, East Kilbride

Red

Red is an apple picked and ready to eat.
Red is lipstick my mum wears at parties.
Red is a water melon with its juicy flesh.
Red are tomatoes, tasty and sweet.
Red is lava spouting from a volcano.
Red is fire from a burning house.
Red is danger on a building site.
Red is a robin that comes in winter.
Red is my bike I ride on every day.
Red is blood from a pinprick.

Ryan Kidd (10)
Greenhills Primary School, East Kilbride

Blue

Blue is like the sky on a nice sunny day.
Blue is like a sapphire shining in the sun.
Blue is like a blueberry ripened and ready to eat.
Blue is like a Slush Puppy that I love to drink.
Blue is my school jumper that I wear every day.
Blue is like chewing gum, chewing in my mouth.
Blue is like my wallpaper I chose for my room.

Callum Thomson (11)
Greenhills Primary School, East Kilbride

Green

Green are the peas that my mum makes me eat.
Green is the school polo shirt that only P7 can wear.
Green are the apples on the tree in the early days of spring
Green is the wet grass early in the morning.
Green is the main colour of my rugby team and it always has been.
Green is the colour of my face when I am jealous.
Green are the trees whispering in the gales.
Green is the wallpaper in my room full of wonderful patterns.

Adam Marshall (10)
Greenhills Primary School, East Kilbride

Happiness

Happiness is red like a juicy strawberry that you can eat.
Happiness sounds like a bird twittering in a very tall tree.
Happiness tastes like a chocolate cake, just coming out of the oven.
Happiness feels like a very soft cloud that I want to sleep on.
Happiness reminds me of my great, great papa.

Rhiannon Braid (7)
Greenhills Primary School, East Kilbride

Night

In my bed I dream about monsters and knights
Fighting dragons and killing them.
In my bed I see lots of colours on my wall
But in daytime there is nothing there.

Lomond Hanson (6)
Guildtown Primary School, Perth

At Night

At night-time the moon shines
Owls say tu-whit tu-whoo,
Falling stars come to my bedroom
Shadows creep inside my curtains
It is very dark and very quiet.

Ellis Martin (6)
Guildtown Primary School, Perth

Night

At night darkness fell on the window in my house
Stars came sparkling in the sky
The sound of an owl flew past my window ledge
I felt scared, then I fell asleep.

Lucy Martin (7)
Guildtown Primary School, Perth

Night

I love the moonlight
I see stars sparkling in the sky.
I see shadows in the dark.
I feel scared.
I hear doors creaking and shutting.
My mum and dad are speaking.
I have scary dreams in my bed.
I hate the dark.

Brad Riley (7)
Guildtown Primary School, Perth

Night

Last night in my bed
I saw a shadow on my curtain
And it made me feel scared.
I heard stamping feet coming up the stairs
A door slamming in the living room
The squeaking of a mouse
Last night in my bed I fell asleep.

Amy Key (6)
Guildtown Primary School, Perth

Night

When it is dark and you think it's night
Owls are hooting, bats are shrieking and squeaking.
Shadows are lurking, night has arrived.
Most children are asleep, all but one
Who didn't go to sleep,
He hears the television on downstairs
Footsteps coming up the stairs,
He drifts to sleep.

Ronan Welch (7)
Guildtown Primary School, Perth

Night

The night sneaks around
The stars peek
The moon comes shining
The night is quiet
In their beds
Children dream of fighting dragons
And being princesses.

Connor O'Malley (6)
Guildtown Primary School, Perth

Sleepy Waves

Waves creeping, then creeping back,
Swishing this way and that.
Teasing me as it rolls on my feet,
The waves laughing as I feel sleepy.
Salty water soothing my feet,
As water goes back I go home.

Emma-Louise Garrow (11)
Hanover Street Primary School, Aberdeen

Life In Weather

Thunder was roaring really loud,
Lightning flashing from the cloud,
The sun is bright, glaring at me,
The snow is ploughing over me.
Wind rushing through the washing rack,
The rain pouring on my back.

Liam Minty 10)
Hanover Street Primary School, Aberdeen

Frequent Flyer

Her first day of work,
Not left in the lurch,
She races to help people
Go on holiday.
Jumping and flying
them to paradise.
Queen of the sky,
Flying like a dream.
The plane,
then glides gently downwards.

Hannah Bettsworth (11)
Hanover Street Primary School, Aberdeen

Earthquake!

There was an earthquake in New York.
He was called Earnest, the earthquake.
He liked to destroy the town.
He thought the Empire State was too showy.
So he ate it and that was the end of it.
Then he stood up and ran home.

Allan Coutts (12)
Hanover Street Primary School, Aberdeen

The Evil Eye

I was outside skipping with my friend,
When the camera caught my eye
I knew it was the end.
They caught me so I told a lie.
The camera's evil eye,
Made me tell a lie.

Laura Minty (10)
Hanover Street Primary School, Aberdeen

Cars, Cars, Cars

Cars, cars, cars all around,
Pick up speed and kill the ground.
Cars, cars, cars tear up tar,
When I get my shiny new car.
Cars, cars, cars burn rubber,
It sticks to the ground like black blubber.

Ross McAllister (12)
Hanover Street Primary School, Aberdeen

Disastrous Fire

The fire laughs, dances and teases me,
Roaring at me and scaring me.
The TV will explode and the Xbox
The fire is bullying me and burning my toys.
The fire is enjoying itself,
The fire is dancing around me.

Stephanie Webster (11)
Hanover Street Primary School, Aberdeen

Golden Boy

God gave me a gift
A gift for me to love
Eyes of blue, golden hair
An angel from above
My baby nephew, Robbie
I do declare.

Caitlin Gemmell (8)
Hareleeshill Primary School, Larkhall

My Young Brother

S cott is stupendous
C aring and kind.
O utside we play football
T raining very, very hard
T en goals are what we scored.

Blue-eyed Scott
Red hair, all short.
Oh he is so funny,
Telling me jokes
Every day I love him more and more
Football is what he loves best.

Kayleigh Gallagher (8)
Hareleeshill Primary School, Larkhall

My Sister, Danielle

S pecial
I love her
S cary
T errific
E nergetic
R ough player

D ancer
A ngel
N ice
I play with her
E very day on our bikes
L ively
L ike her a lot
E veryone loves her.

Sonya Dunnery (8)
Hareleeshill Primary School, Larkhall

At The Beach

At the beach the sun shines bright
We all sleep quietly at night
When we wake up and we play
My mum will say,
'It's time to tidy the room
We will use the broom.'

Heather McLaren (9)
Hareleeshill Primary School, Larkhall

Colours

Gold is for my first ring
Red is for ruby flowers
Green is for shiny grass
Blue is for beautiful sky
Orange is for shining sun
Yellow is for charming daffodils
Brown is for the trunk of a tree.

Ashleigh Yuille (9)
Hareleeshill Primary School, Larkhall

Blistering Winds

Blistering winds can blow you
Strong winds can make you cold
Scorching winds can blow you down
Freezing winds can make you frozen.
But my favourite is a calm wind
Because you don't get cold.

Caitlin Williamson (9)
Hareleeshill Primary School, Larkhall

Fair Trade

Have your chocolate in the day
and you may eat it in any way.
All the chocolate is delicious food
oh, it makes you feel so good.

When I see or hear chocolate
my mouth starts to water for when I eat.
I see the boys, I see the girls
stuffing their faces with Crunchies.

If the poor waste their time
take a fair trade, it's worth it.
But if you don't,
they will never get told.

Just take a fair trade
mainly Divine tastes the same.
So go on, pick up Divine
they will thank you.

Aaron Rossiter (11)
Hatton (Cruden) Primary School, Peterhead

A Pen

A pen is a writing tool of ink
But my pen is different
My pen can take me anywhere I want
To the magical fairies
Or up in space.

My pen can create any character I wish
Crash! What has my pen created?
A giant monster destroying the town
Evil alien zapping houses
Oh no, my pen has run out of ink
I'll simply need a new one.

Hannah Vince (12)
Hatton (Cruden) Primary School, Peterhead

The Suitcase

The suitcase is a mixture of emotions trapped in a steel cage.
The texture is rough like anger or smooth like friendship.
If I ever feel angry with people, the suitcase protects me
from saying things I don't mean.
A suitcase is a hotel for all your clothes to feel safe and warm.
A suitcase is what I use to move from adventure to adventure
or place to place.
They come in different shapes, sizes, patterns and colours.
They are a symbol of friendship, always there for you
and never feel upset or angry.
Suitcases will always be ready and packed with fun, just like me.

Heather Fowlie (11)
Hatton (Cruden) Primary School, Peterhead

Light

A compass directing the way through life
It is illuminating the way to God and eliminating ghostly shadows.

A butterfly, disco dancing, flickering, fluttering,
Lighting up with colourful colours.

A flag, flapping madly in the storm
Big and bold for everyone to see, beckoning safety
With lots of meaning for you and me.

A car letting you travel everywhere
Swerving skilfully with beaming headlights,
Showing you the way through the fog.
Lighting up the speed dial, to stop you getting lost or driving too fast.

Fraser Stevenson (11)
Hatton (Cruden) Primary School, Peterhead

Towel

A towel
big, cuddly, warm and snugly
Wrapped around me
Drying, soothing and comforting
After a hard day.
Suddenly
It becomes a snake
squeezing, squishing, squashing
and squirming me to the ground.
I'm a big blue rug
Being held prisoner
In my own home.
It seems I am under the radiator
It's come from a cold crocodile
to a warm, relaxed towel.
It's starting to cuddle me softly,
I'm getting dry.
No one said I wasn't allowed to cuddle back in comfort.

Jack Mitchell (10)
Hatton (Cruden) Primary School, Peterhead

A Purse

A purse can be a site of wealth and kindness.
A purse can have lots of fun or none.
A purse can be a site of hunger.
A purse can hold cards or money.
A purse can be big or small.
A purse can go anywhere, night or day.
A purse is a rocket, ready for blast-off.
A purse can be the decider on what you buy.
A purse can be black or many more colours.
A purse can be helpful to others.

David Rennie (11)
Hatton (Cruden) Primary School, Peterhead

My Shower

My shower is my own art gallery, with lots of silver patterns.
New Picasso and Leonardo da Vinci paintings with every shower I take.

My shower is my relaxing room, where all my worries get washed away
And where no animals can annoy me.

It is a room of cleanliness, where I get clean.

My shower is my submarine, where it takes me to lots of places.
Oh no, my submarine has a hole in it and water is spraying in
And I'm being sucked out through a whirlpool.

Jemma Douglas (11)
Hatton (Cruden) Primary School, Peterhead

A Watch

It ticks and ticks waiting for something to happen
It sparkles in the dark, dark night
It sets and watches time go by
Shimmering in the light of the sun
Dates and times, people study it
My watch is a toddler, small and it has hands
I like my watch, it's easy to see, though it's getting old
Crunch! Oh no, I stepped on my watch
Oh well, I'll easily get a new one.

Rachael Clark (11)
Hatton (Cruden) Primary School, Peterhead

A Gift

A gift is fantastic when you tear off the wrapper.
It is a toy packed away in an old cupboard.
A gift is for a special occasion.
A gift is love, caring and friendship
A gift is exciting or a piece of treasure
Receiving a gift is best, but giving is better.

Lee Buchan (11)
Hatton (Cruden) Primary School, Peterhead

My Camera

My camera is a carton that captures time and is kept there forever
In a flash, a moment it time stops,
Then carries on after the picture is made.
The picture makes a new land from the past,
While on Earth, time goes on.
My camera will stare at you until in blinks
And you are snatched away from my camera.
On special events, your favourite moments
You want to remember them
Once the pictures have developed,
You will see the smiles and enjoyment you've been looking for.

Holly Gibbon (11)
Hatton (Cruden) Primary School, Peterhead

A Battery

A battery is full of power like a king.
A battery is small and gold and black.
When a battery has too much power
It just takes over the tower.
But when it is put in the huge machine
It drains off all the power
So he is not the king of the tower and he is dead.

Fraser Finnie (10)
Hatton (Cruden) Primary School, Peterhead

Shoes

A treasure chest storing magic and adventure
Waiting to escape at your next spot.
It's a smelly old ogre that gets kept at the door.
It is my flying carpet, speeding me to the astro.
It is my dark spooky cave hiding all my mud and dirt.
Oh, that's me finished my lace, let's go and see where it will take me.

Liam Boyle (11)
Hatton (Cruden) Primary School, Peterhead

My Passport

A passport is a worldwide voucher
With it I can go anywhere
My passport is an aeroplane taking me wherever I wish
Never saying no, only saying come on let's go
My passport is an autobiography about me
Revealing details of my life.

Jack Wright (11)
Hatton (Cruden) Primary School, Peterhead

A Star

A star is a super singer in the night sky.
A star is my mum when she loves me.
A star is my teacher when she is in class.
My dog is a star because she always greets me.
My brother is a star because he always pleases me.
A star is like a magical wishing well that gives me good luck.
A star is what helps us through the dark night sky.
A star is me when I am calm and gentle.

Christopher Reid (11)
Hatton (Cruden) Primary School, Peterhead

A Tap

Turn the golden handle, it screams and screeches
Eek!
Water pours out, it is a serpent slithering down,
then all of a sudden, *bang!*
It is a boiling waterfall, steaming and gushing,
coming out of the tap.
Then it's a monster freezing me
And all this before the bath has begun.

John Paterson (11)
Hatton (Cruden) Primary School, Peterhead

A Fire

A fire is a slithering slimy snake snapping out with poisonous smoke.
A fire is a speeding car destroying everything in its path.
Red-hot flames, a fire is a little child playing with knives.
Bang, boom, blast, a fire is a plane without any wings
crashing into a house.
A fire is a robber stealing our oxygen.

Zander Keith (11)
Hatton (Cruden) Primary School, Peterhead

Autumn

Leaves golden brown, red and blowing in the wind,
The weather gets colder,
The nights get darker,
All the animals get ready to hibernate,
The fireworks cracking and banging in the starlit sky
Purples, greens and reds,
All the farmers gathering in the harvest,
Women making their bread from home-grown grain,
The smell as I walk into the house makes me hungry.

Rebecca Dun (10)
Heriot Primary School, Heriot

It's Time To Go

It's time to go on this crisp autumn night,
Time to go on our long, dark flight.

I can see the small seeds falling softly to the ground
And the colourful leaves twirling round and round.

The celebrations have started and the wonderful sight
The fireworks make as we soar through the night.

And as the dawn rises the sight I can see,
Is the wonderful rivers flowing underneath me.

Hannah Otton (10)
Heriot Primary School, Heriot

The Volcano

The volcano,
Sitting on the flat plains,
Covered in beautiful green vegetation,
A giant termite mound touching the clouds,
A big friendly giant on the face of the world.
Suddenly, a treacherous rumble from the depths of an angry Earth,
The sky goes black as pitch and the ground trembles madly
With the anticipation of the molten lava,
Lava spews out of the tiny vents in the giant, stone skyscraper.
Bang! The summit is destroyed and replaced
With a fountain of orange destruction,
The beautiful trees and plants are now a raging mat of molten rock,
The sun is blocked out with toxic clouds of ash and gas,
A glorious landscape is now covered in hot, thick, oozing slime
Cooling to form a hard rock surface,
But soon the plants will grow back
On the fresh new soil mixed with the ash
And everything will come back just as it was.

Michael Inglis (12)
Heriot Primary School, Heriot

What Love Is

Love moves gracefully in the air
Loves feels soft and smooth
Love tastes beautiful and nice like raspberries growing
Love is pink and red
Love smells like a rose
Love is beautiful
Love looks beautiful
Love can be kept forever
Love is something everybody wants to have
Love is a butterfly flying around my heart
Love is slow and gentle in my heart
Love is like a rose petal.

Charlotte Clark (7)
Heriot Primary School, Heriot

The Snake Of Autumn

When the snake of autumn slithers by,
Leaves are killed by its poisonous breath
And any small animals caught in its way,
Will quickly meet their death.

When the snake of autumn slithers by,
All animals hide away,
The mouse goes to sleep in its hidey-hole
And the squirrel lies down in its drey.

When the snake of autumn slithers by,
It radiates cold from its scales
And however brightly the sun might shine,
It will be to no avail.

When the snake of autumn slithers by,
Its venom drips onto the leaves
And fills them with furious and radiant colour,
But then they fall out of the trees.

When the snake of autumn slithers by,
It feels pity for all it has killed,
So it smothers them over with blankets of leaves,
To ever lie quiet and still.

When the snake of autumn slithers by,
It usually kills off some,
But its rattle is a warning bell,
For winter still to come.

I saw the snake of autumn once:
Its scales were gold, red and brown,
From its mouth came breath and it breathed on the trees
And leaves softly spiralled down.

James Whittaker (10)
Heriot Primary School, Heriot

Fear

Fear looks black
Fear will make you tingle
Fear smells strange and weird
Fear moves with black footsteps
Fear tastes like a sour lemon
Our fear could be a lion
Fear is scary.

William Lawrie (7)
Heriot Primary School, Heriot

Guilt Will Hold On To You Forever

Guilt makes you sorry,
Guilt makes you weep,
It can be quite helpful,
It can help you realise what you have done,
Guilt is not very fun,
Guilt is not what you think,
Guilt will hold on to you forever.

Amy Gilroy (8)
Heriot Primary School, Heriot

Anger

Anger is red, the darkest red
Anger is hard, not squeezy, nor soft, it is dead hard, nothing like it
Anger tastes like blood sauce and a dead mouse
It tastes horrible!
Anger smells like rotten milk that has been spilt and not mopped up
Anger moves fast across the floor, its heart beating like mad
Anger makes you feel like you are going to explode!

Rosa Myers Bradley (7)
Heriot Primary School, Heriot

Love

Love feels very soft
Silky and smooth
Love smells like a flower
It tastes like chocolate too
Love is pink
And that is what I think
Love makes you happy
Or even sad
But most of all
You love each other
And that's all that counts.

Nicola Moffat (8)
Heriot Primary School, Heriot

Anger

Anger looks rough
Anger feels bad and red
Anger smells weird and smoky
Anger moves like a herd of elephants
Anger tastes mouldy and rotten
Anger is a lion, big and strong, eating all the animals.

Beth Whittaker (7)
Heriot Primary School, Heriot

Autumn Is Here Again

It's that time again
The leaves are turning golden brown
All the mice scuttle to find a cosy hole
I'm flying to my winter resort
Sitting on the wire, eating juicy worms
Take-off at last
Coming back in spring.

Jack Morrison (9)
Heriot Primary School, Heriot

Some People . . .

Some people are small
Some people are big
Some people are young
Some people are old
Some people are black
Some people are white
Some people have brown hair
Some people have black hair
Some people are bad
Some people are good
Some people have blue eyes
Some people have brown eyes
But we should all be treated fairly.

Mhairi Finlayson (7)
Heriot Primary School, Heriot

The Corsehope Life

The Corsehope life is great
The wildlife, the shooting, the fishing and the lambing.

It's great seeing all the ewes, their lambs
The sheepdog, Kep, goes mental
He can't wait for the action.

The fishing is great too
Down by the burn, the trout swim by
Just wee tiddlers that will do me.

My dad, he's the gamekeeper
It's fun going shooting after dark
Lamping for foxes
Not many foxes up Corsehope now
It's a great place to live.

Gregor Bell (11)
Heriot Primary School, Heriot

What Is Fear?

Fear is like a quiver in your mouth
Fear puts a shiver up your spine
I would think fear is icy blue
Fear feels like it is sharp
Fear tastes like frozen peas
Fear sounds like an owl in the night sky
Fear makes some people crumple on the floor
Some people enjoy fear and look to do scary things
That is what I think fear is.

Stuart Balfour (8)
Heriot Primary School, Heriot

Hatred Is Disgusting

Hatred looks like oozing blood
Slithering down to the ground
Hatred feels like a big, horrible blob
Glooping and spreading around
Hatred smells like a rotten egg
Fuming and stinking the place
Hatred moves like spilt treacle
Glooping down at a very slow pace.

Peter Starrs (9)
Heriot Primary School, Heriot

Stress Feels Like Chopped Wood

Stress looks like red blood from the heart of Hell
Stress feels like hard, chopped wood
Stress smells like cow dung on a farm
Stress is more like a chainsaw sawing up gravel
Stress tastes like earth and bird droppings in a stew pot
The colour of stress is like black and red demons
Stress leaves you in a knot of pipes on the floor.

Thomas Otton (8)
Heriot Primary School, Heriot

Autumn

Autumn's leaves are falling
In golds and reds and yellows
Swirling to the frosty ground,
Leaving the withered trees
To be blown away by the winds
And crushed underneath the boots of playing children,
But underneath their covered layers
Little beasts hurry by
Everything is preparing
For winter.

The timid little beasts
Stock up on provisions
The birds from the north
Are migrating to the southern, warmer lands
The salmon how they fascinate me
Swimming upstream to the exact place of their birth
Everything is preparing
For winter.

Graham Baxter (11)
Heriot Primary School, Heriot

Goodness

Goodness can be in your heart
Goodness can be in your body
Goodness feels like lovely hot water
Everyone feels goodness
Goodness tastes like great chocolate
Goodness is a nice blue
Everyone feels goodness
Goodness moves like an animal
Goodness smells like a rose
Goodness looks like a little pet
Everyone feels goodness.

Lucy Urquhart (7)
Heriot Primary School, Heriot

In A Shirt Of Scale Mail

Looking round in a world of blue
Lots of rocky castles tilted askew
They provide me with shelter
From predators looking at me
Oh, I hope I don't become their tea
Then I dart, quick and fast
And when I find more shelter
I stop and think, at last.

The sun has blacked out
And I feel at this moment that I could shout
When *whack!* something hits me
I think I'm about become a shark's fish supper tea.

The sea holds many surprises
And you may not always be the one winning the prizes
The sea can be a wonderful place
Just not for the likes of me.

Zac Blake-Campbell (12)
Heriot Primary School, Heriot

What Could I Write?

I am writing a poem for a competition
I wonder what I could write?
Maybe it could be about me riding at the Highland Show
Or maybe about hunting on my pony, Owain
Taking part in a tetrathlon
Sunny, my Shetland pony or my dog, Maggie
I know! I could write about the weather
Or how about my holiday in France
Or maybe about our family holiday in Oasis
I could write about what I am thinking
Yeah! I'll write what I am thinking
Hopefully it will be good.

Charlotte Dun (10)
Heriot Primary School, Heriot

Riding On My Unicorn

I'm riding my beautiful unicorn,
High up in the starry sky,
Trotting quickly over treetops,
Jumping over smoky chimneys.

My unicorn is called Twilight,
She's white with a shimmering horn,
Her mane is soft, her tail is silky,
I love my snow-white unicorn.

We go riding every night-time
When the silver stars are out,
Twilight is enjoying it
She wants to have some fun
So I push my heel into her side.

She's going really fast now,
She's whickering with delight,
I'm laughing while slowing her down
We've had enough,
We're too tired to go on,
To the stable for us,
With a rug and water for Twilight
And hot chocolate for me.

Alice Connor (9)
Heriot Primary School, Heriot

Bonfire Night

On the night of the bonfire,
I feel excited and cold at the same time,
I hear the bonfire crackling,
I feel the fireworks exploding,
The noise running through my body,
I see Guy Fawkes burning in the bonfire,
The stars and the moon shining so bright,
In the darkness of the night.

Greg Crighton (9)
Heriot Primary School, Heriot

My Fluffy Hamster

I have a fluffy hamster,
His name is Furrball.
He'll do anything for a white chocolate button,
Anything at all.

When he grips on tightly,
On the chocolate button.
Lift him up a metre high,
He won't fall.

Even though he's stupid,
He can be very smart.
When I try to pick him up,
To a tube he darts.

Hamster can be vicious,
Very vicious I mean.
They can bite your finger
And make it bleed.

I thought he was very timid,
When I first got him.
But now he comes to me,
Looking for a white chocolate button.

Fiona Inglis (10)
Heriot Primary School, Heriot

The Beach

Just sitting on the bank of the beach
When something caught my eye
A beautiful snow-white horse galloping past me
His mane and tail flying behind him
He ran into the water and disappeared
I thought he had drowned
But after five minutes he came out and ran away
I always look at the spot and hope he's returned.

Naidene Dorman (10)
Heriot Primary School, Heriot

The Rugby Poem

The big game - Scotland Vs Wales
The kick-off starts
The Welsh are right up in the Scottish territory
Try!
The Welsh scorer is Stephen Jones
He takes the conversion
Slots it right through the middle
Now the Scots try to get back in the game
Stephen Jones passes to Gareth Thomas
Interception from Chris Paterson
And the Scots score a try!
The full time while blows
The Welsh have won - 28 points to 18.

Keith Young (10)
Heriot Primary School, Heriot

Fishing

Waiting, waiting, waiting,
I'm bored and annoyed,
The man beside me has caught five fish.

I've caught none,
I've been fishing for two hours,
Without any results,
Casting again and again and again,
Reeling in the shiny lure,
Watching it flash through the water,
Then *whack!*

I've landed a fish!
Excited and satisfied,
The wait has been worth it.

Tenzin Stephen (10)
Heriot Primary School, Heriot

A White Horse

In a forest I see a white horse
That shines like the moon
Galloping up and down
Jumping over a hundred logs
Doing no harm to the creatures below
It's nice to see it free.

I would take good care of it myself
If I was allowed
I would stand staring at it for ages
Till the breeze came, the trees would rustle, owls hoot.

The white horse in the shelter lying down, asleep
Its mane and tail waving in the breeze
It looks lonely and lost and I want to help
But I woke up and it was all a dream
Thank goodness for that!

Katie Louise Dun (9)
Heriot Primary School, Heriot

Helping

I like helping people
If you stay near me and you need help
Give me a call
I will be round, on your doorstep
As soon as you put the phone down.

I will do the work
In five minutes flat
And out of the house
Before you know it.

Katrina Nicol (9)
Heriot Primary School, Heriot

The Greatest Wrestlers Of The World

Boogie man, Boogie man
What terrors will he bring?
His finishing move is simple
It's called 'pump handle swing'
Boogie man, Boogie man

Undertaker, Undertaker
What terrors will he bring?
His finishing move is simple
It's called 'choke ring'
Undertaker, Undertaker

Kurt Angle, Kurt Angle
What terrors will he bring?
His finishing move is simple
It's called 'Angle sling wing'
Kurt Angle, Kurt Angle.

Paige Orr (9)
Highlanders Academy Primary School, Greenock

Fear

One night we heard
Squealing and howling
It sounded like werewolves
And squeaking doors!

And the taste of it
Was blood
And it smelt like smelly old socks
And the sewers!

And there were shadows
Of people getting killed!
It felt windy and scary
And reminds me of bad dreams.

Scott Anderson (9)
Highlanders Academy Primary School, Greenock

All About Cake

Cake, cake, cake
How do you make?
Cake, cake, cake
How do you make?

Add sugar, icing, flour
Then make it into a tower
Sugar, icing, flour
Give it lots of power!

Cake tastes good
Just like other food
Cake is the best
Because it lives in the west.

Cake is great on your birthday
And it tastes lovely!
If you like cake
Just start to make and bake!

Eoin Cole (9)
Highlanders Academy Primary School, Greenock

My Duckling, Bob

My duckling, Bob
Should get a job
He hit his head
On a brass doorknob

That's my duckling, Bob!

My duckling, Bob
Asked me this . . .
'Why are girls always sad?'
Maybe because they smell real bad!

Robbie Philip (10)
Highlanders Academy Primary School, Greenock

Another Long Day

Rise and shine
It's nearly nine.
Rules in school
Are so not cool.

In the playground
It starts to rain
Getting wet
Is such a pain.

Some pupils think
Their teachers . . .
When they shout
Are scary creatures.

At dinnertime
We have our lunch
Because we all
Like to munch!

Some of the pupils
Like to skive
They've done it
Since they arrived!

Mondays and Wednesdays
We do our gym
Keeping fit -
Can keep you slim.

The pupils sometimes act really dull
Because they can't get things in their skull
Some of the pupils think they are dumb
Now and then they are a pain in the bum.

It's three o'clock so give a cheer
Hometime is nearly here!

Nathan Cory (9)
Highlanders Academy Primary School, Greenock

My Brother

Lee is my brother
My brother is he
He's tall and skinny
And always shouts at me

My brother thinks I'm stupid
My brother thinks I'm daft
But he is the only one
That looks like a giraffe

His feet are always smelly
It makes me always hold my nose
Will he ever smell sweet?
Oh goodness, who knows!

After all he is my brother
And I will never forget him
But the one thing to remember
I will always love him.

Amanda Cochrane (9)
Highlanders Academy Primary School, Greenock

My Dog, Sandy

When I went to my gran's
I went to see Sandy
I liked to play catch the ball
And eat lots of candy

One sad Thursday
When we were out to play
Old Sandy died
And everyone cried

I wish for just one day
Sandy could come and play
Then I would not be so sad
I would remember him and feel glad.

Shaun MacDonald (8)
Highlanders Academy Primary School, Greenock

Friendship

Friendship is like whistling and laughing
Friendship is like red for roses and yellow for brightness
Friendship is like a bird singing and the sun shining
But nothing can take that away.

Friendship is like baking a cake
Friendship is like making a card
Friendship is like a red, red rose blowing in the breeze
But nothing can take that away.

Friendship isn't like dying
Friendship isn't like crying
Friendship is such like smiling
Friendship is such like styling
But nothing can take that away.

Nothing really matters when it comes to friendship
And nothing can take that away
That's right . . . nothing can take that away!

Chantelle Lafferty (9)
Highlanders Academy Primary School, Greenock

Dancing Homework

My dancing homework
It dances all around
It's got a crazy beat
And a magic sound

It's so cool
Being out of school
My mum's not got a clue
If she finds out
She'll get the blues

I'm trying my best
Not to get depressed
Homework's not bad
But sometimes makes me sad.

Liam McBride (9)
Highlanders Academy Primary School, Greenock

Friendship

Friendship is like the colour of
Pink and purple!

Friendship sounds like
A bird tweeting - *tweet, tweet!*
Someone laughing soundly
Really . . . it's a little girl singing!

It tastes like a super fairy cake
Mmm! Mmm!
It's like a baked fairy cake
The one I love the best!

It feels fun in my eyes
I can see me having fun
Friendship is getting stronger!

My life with friends
Can this moment last longer!
Friendship! Friendship!

Having fun, laughing
And giggling with joy . . . oh please!
Let friendship get stronger!

Shari Williamson (9)
Highlanders Academy Primary School, Greenock

Dream

I feel locked in my room, all snug in my bed
Like a mummy in a tomb with a bad, bed head
People think I'm weird but they don't know my dreams
Dreams of them with a beard, eating summer creams

I feel like I'm in the sky, I think I am asleep
I don't think it's a lie then my alarm goes *beep, beep, beep*
I was looking for my dog, I forgot she passed away
Eating chocolate log she always got her way!

This poem is the story of . . . a dream
But there is more . . .

I wish my dog Frosty could last forever
But then she sadly passed away
I could smell her wet fur and taste metallic blood
Now she can always stay

I could see Frosty's shadow
Her shadow hovering in the distance
She wasn't allowed in Haddows
Loved marshmallows but could never resist them

Sadness feels like Frosty's fur although it's soft and lovely
She could never be a cat that would purr, but she still is lovely
Sadness isn't like a red, red rose that blows in the breeze
Sadness is such a dead, dead rose that got caught in a tree.

Hollie Fyfe (9)
Highlanders Academy Primary School, Greenock

My Pink And Yellow Friend

Pink and yellow
Pink and yellow
The sun came up in
His little yellow way
His little yellow way

Pink and yellow
Pink and yellow
The ice cream came up
And said, 'Hello, hello!'
And said, 'Hello, hello!'

Pink and yellow and blue
The sky went up in
His little blue way
His little blue way

Pink and yellow and blue
The colours are up to you
Pink and yellow and blue
The colours are up to you!

Erin Oribine (9)
Highlanders Academy Primary School, Greenock

Giraffes!

Giraffes pink, green and purple and red
There must be something going on in my head!

As I went to bed I said
Pink, green, purple and red
There must be something
Going on in my head!

I woke up in the morning
Found I had a bump on my head
So giraffes pink, green, purple and red
Was only in my head!

Hannah McBain (9)
Highlanders Academy Primary School, Greenock

The Cat In The Hat

He's the cat in the hat
There's no doubt about that
He's always late
For an important date

His friends are fools
They play with power tools
He's so crazy
And his friends are lazy

When there is a mouse in the house
He acts like a big girl's blouse
Every time it's sunny
He is really funny

And now you all know
He's the cat in the hat!

Kaleb McGartland (9)
Highlanders Academy Primary School, Greenock

Anger

Anger makes me hear lots of noises
Like shouting, screams and crying
I think it means someone is dying
Maybe anger means something is frying.

Anger makes my most horrible food and drink
Taste bloody and dusty
Once anger made me turn rusty
Then I saw a skull and it made me shiver worse still!

When I was in pain, anger made it rain
I saw some bones and heard some moans
All I can smell is fire and smoke!

Anger I do not like it
You can't see it and you don't know
When it will come!
All it reminds me of is my little brother!

Nathan O'Neill (9)
Highlanders Academy Primary School, Greenock

Roses Are Red, Violets Are Blue

Roses are red,
Violets are blue,
Sugar is sweet
And so are you.

That's what most
People say to you
On Valentine's Day,
Most people say,
Do you love me?
Because I love you!

Love sometimes looks
Like a big red rose,
But sometimes that's
Not the way it goes.

Love is nice,
Like tiny mice,
They're OK as long as it's not a rat,
Or I would need a lot of cats.

That is the way it goes.

Lauren Nelson (8)
Highlanders Academy Primary School, Greenock

Fear

Fear, fear
Reminds me of
Spiders

Fear, fear
Reminds me of
crabs

Fear, fear
Reminds me of
My mum

Fear, fear
Reminds me of
My dad

Fear, fear
Reminds me of
Ghosts

Fear, fear
Reminds me of
Sharks

Fear, fear
Reminds me of
Midges

Fear, fear
Reminds me of
Killer whales

Fear, fear
Reminds me of
The big, deep sea!

Dean Munro (9)
Highlanders Academy Primary School, Greenock

Cakes

Creamy, dreamy chocolate cake,
That's what I want,
So that's what I'll bake.

I'll add the sugar, the cocoa,
Next the butter,
Then yum, yum, yum
I will mutter . . .
Then . . .
Raspberry cheesecake,
I'll turn on the oven,
One hundred and eighty degrees
And when it's ready
I'll add the cheese.

It's simple really,
How to bake;
A book and ingredients,
That's all it takes.

I'm still hungry now,
I've had my dinner,
I'll wait five minutes,
For the custard to simmer.

I've poured the custard over the cakes,
I'm eating them now,
I'm so happy I baked.

Linsay Shaw (10)
Hill of Beath Primary School, Cowdenbeath

The Boy From Allan Park

Once, there was a boy from Allan Park
Who was very scared of the pitch-black dark
He ate a carrot
And turned into a parrot
Now he lives with a mouse who owns his house.

Reece Smith (10)
Hill of Beath Primary School, Cowdenbeath

What Do I Care?

There's a rocket in your pocket
What do I care?

There's thread on your head
What do I care?

There's a rose up your nose
What do I care?

There's a monster behind you
What do I . . .

Greig Mair (10)
Hill of Beath Primary School, Cowdenbeath

The Sad And Happy Poem

I feel giggly when my dad tickles me,
I feel proud when I pass my reading test,
I feel overjoyed when it is Christmas Day,
I am excited when I get my white belt,
I feel happy that I have three friends,
I get terrified when the door is closed,
I feel down when I think about my mum.

Daniel Dalton (7)
Holy Family Primary School, Broxburn

Sad And Happy

I feel sad when I think of my granda,
I get scared when the lights go out at night,
I get bored when I have no one to play with,
I feel happy when my friends can play with me,
I am overjoyed when it is Christmas morning,
I feel upset when there is nothing to do,
I feel happy when it is my birthday party.

Sean Coyle (7)
Holy Family Primary School, Broxburn

Night The Lurker

Night is a young woman
Who grieves
For she slays Day
She lives in a large, dark house
Gloom sweeps her corridors
Her garden is dead
The trees resemble scarecrows
Her eyes are as silver as a crescent moon

She is as elusive as storm clouds
An army clad in shadows follows her
Her cloak dominates all light
She moves swiftly and silently
She preys on the unsuspecting

Be careful
She's dangerous.

Jamie Griffiths (11)
Holy Family Primary School, Broxburn

I Feel

I felt proud when I had to perform to some people,
I felt shocked at Christmas opening presents,
I get excited when I go to M&D's park,
I am thrilled when I get a sleepover with friends,
I was sad when my fish died in the fish tank,
I feel guilty when I tell a lie to my mum,
I felt terrified when I was on a roller coaster,
I get upset when my dad leaves to go to work.

Shauna Green (8)
Holy Family Primary School, Broxburn

The Dread Of Night

Night is a serial killer
He makes me feel scared
His face looks straight
His eyes are serious
His mouth you can't see
His hair you can't see
A balaclava covers them both
His clothes are made of dark black-ribbed nylon
He moves slickly
He speaks harshly
He lives on a houseboat
With broken and smashed windows
Night frightens me.

Sean Finnigan (9)
Holy Family Primary School, Broxburn

My Feelings

I feel overjoyed when my sister comes to stay,
I get excited when I think about babies,
I feel proud when I get to the finish line,
I feel giggly when I look at my brother.

I felt shocked when my sister broke some bad news,
I get scared when my brother shouts loudly,
I feel lifeless when I am ill at my house,
I am down when I miss my big sister,
I felt heartbroken when my first cat died.

Iona O'Hanlon (8)
Holy Family Primary School, Broxburn

Night

Night is a Grim Reaper
He makes me feel scared
His body is bony and slouched
He is so scary
He is like a person walking towards you with a knife
Trying to kill you
His eyes are like flames
And he wears a large, ripped black cloak
He's got no hair whatsoever
He carries a large stick, with a hooked knife on top
He lives in a dark, gloomy and slimy house
With a ghost dog and a skeleton wife
Night scares me.

Aidan Brown (9)
Holy Family Primary School, Broxburn

Night

Night is like my best friend
She makes me feel joyful and safe
Her face is pretty and friendly
Her eyes are moonlight-blue
She has a small pale pink mouth
Silky brown is the colour of her hair
The material of her clothes is starry and shiny
She moves silently and gracefully
Her voice is quiet and peaceful
She lives in a small cottage all alone
I love Night and Night loves me!

Ashleigh Gorman (10)
Holy Family Primary School, Broxburn

I Feel

I felt scared when I started Cubs at night,
I get bored when I am sleeping in my bed,
I am tired when I wake up in the morning,
I feel angry when my sisters annoy me,
I feel lifeless when I am sick and ill,
I feel embarrassed when I make big mistakes,
I felt sad when my aunty Florence died,
I feel proud when I achieve things,
I feel at home after my work,
I feel shocked when I have a surprise.

Ciaran Reddington (8)
Holy Family Primary School, Broxburn

My Feelings

I feel excited when it's Christmas Day,
I am glad when my gran comes to stay,
I feel happy when I see my tall dad,
I am always giggly when people tickle me,
I get embarrassed when tall people tease me,
I get terrified when it is very dark,
I get very hot when I get into bed,
I feel very sad when my friends are not in.

Caitlin Reddington (7)
Holy Family Primary School, Broxburn

School - Haiku

Maths, art, French and gym
Educational they are
So let's learn away.

Kara Bradbeer (10)
Inverkeithing Primary School, Inverkeithing

Recipe For Summer

Take a blazing sun
Maybe a sandy beach
Get some T-shirts and shorts
Some sandals too
Pour in a swimming pool
So that you can get cool
Also a freezing drink
Don't forget the ice
Mix in some sun lotion
To keep you from sunburn
Add a seat so that you can relax
Don't get dehydrated
Enjoy!

Gemma Park (10)
Inverkeithing Primary School, Inverkeithing

Colours

There are so many different colours
Gold is really shiny like the sun
Silver is shiny like the moon
Orange is cheerful and bright
Blue is the colour of my eyes
Purple is my favourite colour
Rose is nearly pink
Red is really bright
Violet is darker than purple
Aqua is like light green
Black is so strong
Lime is quite light.

Morgan Henderson (10)
Inverkeithing Primary School, Inverkeithing

The Volcano

The volcano lies dead,
Dead for 100 years,
The volcano stands proud,
Proud like a castle or king.

The volcano is dangerous,
Dangerous like an angry tiger,
The volcano is hot,
Hot like the boiling sun,
The volcano is angry,
Angry like a villain.

The volcano has exploded,
Exploded like a meteor,
The volcano sprays out lava,
Like a fiery shower of rain,
It flows down the mountains,
Like a carpet of fire.

Abby Drummond (10)
Inverkeithing Primary School, Inverkeithing

Oh, Summer Tree

Oh, summer tree
How beautiful you look to me
With all your green leaves shining
You shade me from the red-hot summer sun
You bring music to my ears
With your beautiful rustling tunes
Your muscular branches are good to swing from
You are as tall as a house and as strong as a brick
Oh, summer tree.

Jay James Moir (10)
Inverkeithing Primary School, Inverkeithing

The Sea

The sea is a big dog
A big black dog
That wants its dinner
And won't rest till it gets it.

Then the sun comes out
And the sea is calm
Like a fluffy brown teddy bear
That everyone wants to hug.

Derri Barron (10)
Inverkeithing Primary School, Inverkeithing

The Sea Dog

The sea is like a hungry dog
It was grabbing at the sand
Trying to eat the sea
The sea has giant jaws
Leaving shells beyond it
Washing away all the sand.

Linzi Simpson (10)
Inverkeithing Primary School, Inverkeithing

Puma - Haiku

A puma can pounce
Over big rocks and puddles
It is very smart.

Neil Trebble (11)
Inverkeithing Primary School, Inverkeithing

The River

The river's bed
Is as soft as a sponge
The river flows
Like a winding snake through the hills.

The river can be
Angry like a tiger
Ready to pounce
On its prey.

It is as beautiful
As a model
Strolling down the catwalk
When the sun hits it
It glitters in its beauty.

So now you know
The river
Has a side of kindness
Anger and beauty.

Daniel Richards (10)
Inverkeithing Primary School, Inverkeithing

The Bright Sun - Haiku

The sun shines brightly
Over us all every day
We enjoy it so.

Moira MacMillan (11)
Inverkeithing Primary School, Inverkeithing

Red

Red is anger storming away
Red is a sparkling ruby
Red is like a volcano exploding
Red is one of my favourite colours.

Red is a magic unicorn's horn
Red is like the sun melting through you!
Red is a mighty lion
Red is a dragon's eye.

Red puts a quiver down my back
Red is a beautiful rose
Red is a spicy red pepper
Red is hot!

Emma Johnson (10)
Inverkeithing Primary School, Inverkeithing

Recipe For Spring

Take some lovely sun
Take two small leaves
Maybe a bit of light nights
Add some strong bark
And mix it all together
For ten minutes carefully
Then take some great clouds
Pour in some singing birds
Add a petal or two
Then mix it again
And then, you are finished.

Melissa Black (10)
Inverkeithing Primary School, Inverkeithing